Marion Thrasher

A History of the Thrasher Family

Traced through the Eighteenth and Nineteenth Centuries in England and America

Marion Thrasher

A History of the Thrasher Family
Traced through the Eighteenth and Nineteenth Centuries in England and America

ISBN/EAN: 9783337213091

Printed in Europe, USA, Canada, Australia, Japan

Cover: Foto ©ninafisch / pixelio.de

More available books at **www.hansebooks.com**

A HISTORY

of

THE THRASHER FAMILY

Traced Through

THE EIGHTEENTH AND NINETEENTH CENTURIES

in

ENGLAND AND AMERICA

By Dr. Marion Thrasher
San Francisco, California
1895

INTRODUCTORY

It may seem strange that a resident upon the Pacific Coast should attempt to write the history of a family, found for the most part upon the Atlantic Slope, and in the States east of the Rocky Mountains. But the writer has resided in many of the Eastern and Middle States, and for years has been tracing the history of this family, whose name he bears. In publishing this genealogical work, letters have been written to England, and to almost every State in the Union.

Wherever we have heard of a Thrasher, from the epitaph of a tombstone in a lonely country village to a name found in a City Directory of a great metropolitan centre, we have followed him with a sleuth hound's perseverance, usually until our purpose was accomplished. We have not discovered a Thrasher, but that could be traced to one of the three original brothers that settled at Redstone, Maryland, in 1750.

We can carry for decades back the standard and throughbred horse, through annals carefully chronicled, and why should not a human family however humble, deserve as much consideration? Though we trace our ancestral lineage to a king or a peasant, to a philosopher or a fool, to a priest or a criminal, in any case we can secure much material for profitable study. Family pride is the common heritage of civilized men, and the perusal of our ancestral biography is the most fascinating of all literature. The memoirs collated in this book have been secured from personal interviews, Bible records, epistolary correspondence, from newspapers and biographical dictionary, and in the main are believed to be correct. If I have given more in detail my own branch of the family, than any other, it is only because I have had better opportunity of securing information.

January 1, 1895

Marion Thrasher, A.M., M.D.,
1228 Market Street, San Francisco,
California,

THE FAMILY NAME

Some centuries since in England, as well as in other parts of the Old World, trades descended from father to son, from son to grandson-- indeed, for generations the same vocation was followed.

If a tailor, carpenter or shoemaker; that became the generic name. To others, some striking peculiarity they possessed would suggest a name, that would be given. John was seldom heard in England before the Norman conquest, but afterwards became quite common, because of the popularity of King John.

Thrasher might have had its origin from two sources, viz.: from some of the early ancestors being executioners to flay criminals with the knout, and thus receiving the name of Thrasher--or to some ancestor who had gained a name as pugilist, and was known and feared, possibly, as a Thrasher. In England, following the Middle Ages, this was a common method of receiving the surname. Probably this peculiarity of some remote ancestor, originated this family name, now rather widely scattered over the earth. We are led to accept this hypothesis for the reason that the Thrashers as a rule are strong, athletic men, and almost universally long lived, which is an evidence of great vitality. The founder of the family as I have traced it, Thomas Thrasher, died in his ninety-ninth year. Many of the name have distinguished themselves for their courage.

JOHN THRASHER (1730-1806) was a Revolutionary soldier, known for his bravery and daring.

JOSIAH THRASHER (1763-1849), though a cripple, fought from horseback in the early Indian wars of Kentucky, and tradition says sent more than one redskin to his happy hunting ground.

STEPHEN THRASHER (1760-1833) as Major of Kentucky troops in the war of 1812 evinced conspicuous courage.

WILLIAM P. THRASHER (1818-1862) fell mortally wounded while fighting before Winchester on that memorable August 30, 1862.

Dr. D. W. Scott of McDonough, Ga., whose mother was a Thrasher, writes me: "The Thrashers are a high-minded, honorable people, quick to resent an insult--in other words, good fighters, when that was the order of the day."

For centuries Great Britain has been the home of the family. They may be found today scattered here and there in England, Ireland, Wales. Mr. Thrasher, a well-known Magistrate, now officiates in the Law Chambers at Liverpool. At Belfast, Ireland, a Judge Thrasher lives, while in Wales reside gentleman farmers by that name. John S. Thrasher, the traveler, historian and journalist, once told the writer that he had found the name of Thrasher on tombstones in the Strand--in the heart of London. He told the Hon. Stephen Thrasher of Mississippi, so the latter writes: "That he had traveled through England looking over records to trace, as far as he could, the history of the name, and had found many in the ministry and among the middle classes, but none among the nobility." This would seem to verify my hypothesis concerning the origin of the name.

M. T.

PART FIRST
1725-1824   1729-1806

THOS. THRASHER ------------ MARTHA THRASHER

(Both born in Wales, England.)

FIVE CHILDREN.

BENJAMIN THRASHER 1758   JOHN THRASHER 1761-1840
MARY THRASHER   1760   ELIAS THRASHER 1767
        HENRIETTA THRASHER (born in Virginia) 1769

These Bible records were sent me by Mrs. William Thrasher of Lewisport, Kentucky, who copied them from an old family Bible that had been handed down through generations.

THOMAS THRASHER (1725-1824), the eldest of three brothers--the other two being John and William, was born in Wales, England, October 29, 1725. But little is known of his parents, except that they were endowed with health and considerable wealth. His ancestors undoubtedly possessed great physical vitality, for Thomas Thrasher died in 1824, nearly a century old. He married Martha (her maiden name is unknown) on April 21, 1748, on her nineteenth birthday, she having been born on April 21, 1729. We have the record of five children having been born to them, viz.: Benjamin Thrasher, born 1758; Mary Thrasher, born January 28, 1760; John Thrasher, born February 16, 1761, married in 1890; Elias Thrasher, born May 4, 1767; Henrietta Thrasher, born February 14, 1769, died May 8, 1821. From their marriage in 1748 to the birth of Benjamin in 1758, was ten years, but no record could be found chronicling any births during these years. He with his two other brothers emigrated, and came to Redstone, Maryland, in about the year 1750. We know it was prior to 1769, for on January 23rd of that year Josiah Thrasher, the great grandfather of the writer, was born to John Thrasher (Thomas Thrasher's younger brother) who a year previous had married Elizabeth Hooker. Again we know it was prior to 1767, for Elias Thrasher, Thomas' fourth child, was born on May 4, 1767, in Virginia, after Thomas had left Maryland, and taken up his residence in that state.

It was before 1761 even, for in that year John Thrasher, the third child, was born in Virginia, and subsequently became the founder of that name in Georgia. Benjamin, Mary and Henrietta Thrasher, children of Thomas Thrasher, we have been unable to trace, but according to Stephen Thrasher, Benjamin probably settled in Florida. John Thrasher (1761-1840), the third child, moved to Clark County, Georgia, at an early day, probably just after the Revolution. His great grandson, Dr. D. W. Scott of McDonough, Georgia, gives me a history of this John Thrasher, and his descendants, which I give.

                    1761-1840
        JOHN THRASHER---------------- ---------SUSAN BARTON
                        Ten Children
INFANT died 1788   DAVID 1796-1882
BARTON 1790   SUSAN 1801-1892
RUTH 1792   JOHN 1800
ELIZABETH 1793   FRANCES 1802
ISAAC 1794-1878   MARY 1804

John Thrasher, 1761-1840, and his descendants in Georgia. Compiled by Dr. D. W. Scott, of McDonough, Ga.

Dr. Marion Thrasher, San Francisco.

Dear Sir: I now proceed to give you the history of the Thrasher Family in Georgia. Family tradition says the family first located in Maryland and then moved to West. John Thrasher who moved to Clark County, Ga., judging from natural events, must have been born about 1761, A. D., and died perhaps about 1840. He married a Miss Susan Barton, whose father was killed by the Indians in Daniel Boone's first expedition into Kentucky. His wife died first. John Thrasher died at his son-in-law's, Joe Hugheys, and was buried, I think, in Clark County, Ga., now Oconee, a new county made from Clark and Morgan Counties. John Thrasher and Susan Barton had born unto them ten children. The oldest daughter died in infancy. The second, a son named Barton Thrasher (1790) married a lady named Miss Frances Otes. The third, a daughter, named Ruth Thrasher, married Robert Trimble. The fourth, a son named Isaac Thrasher, married Miss Elizabeth Hester. The fifth, a son, named David Thrasher, born the twenty-fifth of February, 1796, married Miss Mary Hughey, born September 7, 1798, died May 25, 1863. She was a distant relative of Jefferson Davis, President of the Southern Confederacy. The sixth, a daughter, named Susan Thrasher, 1798, married Joseph Hughey. The seventh, a son named John Thrasher, married Miss* Elizabeth Mitchell. The eighth, a daughter named Frances Thrasher, 1802, married Fletcher Foster. The ninth, a daughter named Mary Thrasher, married Anderson Middlebrooks.

Barton Thrasher, 1790, and Mary Oats, lived in Clark County near Farmington, now Oconee County, raised seven children, four boys and three girls. The eldest child named Early Thrasher, married Mary Hester. His wife died leaving him four children; two of his sons were named Barton and Albert Thrasher, lawyers, who at one time lived in Atlanta, Ga., and practiced their profession there. Albert married a Miss Hayden of that city, both immigrated to Florida a few years since. Early Thrasher afterwards married a Miss Brooks. He died about 1879 in Florida; his widow is still living. Barton's second child, a daughter named Susan, married Dr. Lewis Anderson; She raised two sons, Barton and James, who live in Madison, Morgan County, Ga. She died about 1864. The third, a son named Jack Thrasher, married Marion Williams. He died about 1850, A. D., leaving a widow and two children, a son and daughter. His son died while young, his daughter is still living. Her name is Josephine; she married her cousin, Barton Overby. She lives at Farmington, Oconee County, Ga. The fourth child, a son named John Thrasher, never married, and died about 1879. The fifth child, a daughter, named Cora Thrasher, married Basil Overby, a prominent lawyer of Atlanta, Ga. He ran for Governor of Georgia, on the Temperance ticket, but was defeated. The sixth child, a son, named Barton Thrasher, married, but I do not remember the name. He died in 1860, childless. The seventh child, a girl, named Frances, married William Anderson. She and her husband both died about one year after marriage.

Ruth Thrasher 1792, married Robert Trimble, raised six children—three sons and three daughters. Their son Albert Trimble, lived to be about fifty years old. He never married. John Trimble married Victori Simmons, died about 1854, A. D. Eliza Trimble married William Jackson, raised two children, the oldest a daughter, Susan Jackson, married Dr. Parks. Her son's name is Barton Jackson. The mother and daughter are both dead. Barton Jackson is still living in Jackson County, Ga., near Wilder. Susan Trimble married, but I forget her name. Amanda Trimble married Benjamin Fuller.

*Emera Ann Elizabeth Mitchell, dau. of Dr. Thomas Mitchell and Mary Hood Mitchell, in Montgomery Co., Ala., on Jan. 14, 1826

sher, 1793, third child of John Thrasher, married Green
ve daughters. Her oldest daughter, Permalia, married
ie died a few years ago. Her children live near Alpha-
ond daughter, Susan Reynolds, married William Robertson.
:, A. D. Some of her children I think live in Newton
social Circle. The third daughter, Lutitia Reynolds,
irn, and lived in Congers, Ga. She died in 1886, A. D.
Mrs Jack Pierce, living in Congers, Ga., and several
: fourth child, named Eliza Reynolds, married a man by
The fifth child, Caroline Reynolds, married Isaac Weaver.
: a number of years ago.
' 1794, married Elizabeth Hester; reared six children--
laughters. The oldest girl's name I forget. She married
. She died about 1846, A. D. Second child, Barton
i Miss Elder, and had four sons. B. E. Thrasher, of
and a prominent man. I. C. Thrasher, (farmer). T. H.
i physician of standing), and G. B. Thrasher, of Beatty-
ster in the Baptist Church, of more than ordinary ability.
William Thrasher, married I forget whom. Fourth child,
ed a Mr. Whitlock, and lived in Clark County, Ga. Fifth,
irasher, a Methodist preacher, married Miss Annett Row-
ing the late war and left three children, two sons and
oldest son named Alonzo Thrasher; second son named
good boy of high standing. He was killed in Farmington,
, while attending school, by a son of Dr. Price. The
i; to whom I don't know. Sixth son of Isaac Thrasher
n, died in the war of the Confederacy; left a widow and
id Thrasher, (1796-1882), the fifth son of John Thrasher,
Hughey, of Morgan County, Ga., twenty-fifth of Jan., 1816.
r, was born January 25, 1796; died June 7, 1882. David
Hughey had fourteen children born unto them, seven sons
s. The eldest son was named:.
Thrasher, born November 17, 1816, A. D., married Miss
d raised seven children--four sons and three daughters,
id and William, Bethuel, Fannie and Ellen were their
the second time to Mrs Tresvant of Lake City, Fla. His
s in Lake City, Fla. The second child of David Thrasher,
rasher, (called "Cousin John,") on account of his libera-
of heart, was born February 24, 1818, A. D., and married
, of Fulton County, Ga. He is the "Cousin John" Thrasher
st house in Atlanta, Ga., that had a plank floor in it,
yard of calico ever sold in Atlanta. He Contributed
ction of the first Baptist Church, which is an elegant
d now has for its pastor Rev. J. B. Hawthorne, a man of
on in the South as a pulpit orator. He and his wife
y, and with a lavish hand and in regal style. They raised
ur sons and three daughters. He is still living at the
City, Pasco County, Fla., and is the oldest living des-
rasher and Susan Barton, and is considered one among the
en living. He will leave a good and bright record in
ife is as generous and kind woman as ever lived. They
loved and respected by all that know them. "Cousin John,"
ted considerable wealth in Atlanta, which was mostly
war. He represented his County in the Legislature of the
n Thrasher had eight children, viz., Jessie S., born

4-a)
The following information was obtained from the "THRASHER" genealogical record on file in the Georgia Department of Archives and History, in Atlanta, Georgia, and fills in the missing data from this book:

BLS (who had six children: Paul, Silas, Mary A., Anna, Maggie and Ruth); Horton C., David O., Willis Adger, John J. (died at nine), Margaret V., Mary D., Ellen F. (dead). His oldest son, Jessie S. Thrasher, is in the mercantile business at Chattanooga, Tennessee. Conway Turton Thrasher, . B. Thrasher, sons of his, are fruit growers and farmers at Dade City, Florida. David Olivor Thrasher, ex-judge, Attorney at Law, Dade City, Fla. His oldest daughter, Eugenie (Jesse writes me that her name is Margaret Virginia - Ed.) married a Mr. Earnest; Mamie married a Floridian, and Ellen a Dr. Torry.

- -

The following added January 1, 1936 by John James Carnott, Nashville, Tennessee:

John James Thrasher died November 13, 1899, and is interred Dade City, Florida (Pasco Co.). Some 40 years ago he returned to Atlanta for a reunion with his fellow pioneer citizens -- Wash Collier of Collier grazing fame and George W. Adair, capitalist. The Atlanta Constitution devoted a couple of full columns with pictures of the trio, and much about the early experiences, including the story about the time "Cousin " John needed a foreman for some construction work and located his man over in Carolina, but the man would not agree to come unless his wife could accompany him; the man's wife would only agree to come over provided a plank floor was put in the house, so "Cousin" John went to ask Collier who then was conducting a sawmill and secured slabs to build the first puncheon floor in an Atlanta residence. When it was completed the foreman's wife gave a "ball" and "Cousin John", wearing high heeled Spanish boots, had the first dance with the lady. One of the heels got caught in the floor and was pulled off, but nevertheless "Cousin John" continued the dance.

Although he accumulated considerable wealth, he never disowned his kin; in fact a cousin down in Alabama, hearing of his wealth, sent his two daughters on an ox-cart, with a brindle ox and a bale of cotton, to the Atlanta market. When they reached Atlanta several offered to buy their cotton, but they insisted on locating "Cousin" John Thrasher. The curious ones followed the girls to see what John Thrasher would do and say. He came out of his store, stepped upon the cart, addressing the curious ones: 'I know why you are here, you think you will see John Thrasher disown his kin, but gentlemen the purest blood flows through their veins and any of you should feel very highly honored, and justly proud, if you too, as I do, could claim them for your kin. I am indeed fortunate, etc., etc. - -

The young ladies went into the store, picked out about $1,00 (probably 15.00) worth of goods, and when they asked the amount of their bill, "Cousin" John said: 'Ain't you my kin?' -- you owe me nothing.' But, the young ladies insisted, went down in their secret pocket, pulled out a bag of gold and paid their bill.

(4-b)

"Another, and more recent writeup of Atlanta's pioneer merchants appeared in the Atlanta Journal, under date of Sunday, September 15th, 1935, reading in part:

"To John Thrasher, familiarly known as "Cousin John", belonged the honor of erecting the first store near the site of Terminus, in 1839, the settlement which later became Atlanta. The store was built on the ground now occupied by the Federal Reserve Bank, where for so many years the First Presbyterian Church was situated. Cousin John had associated with him a man by the name of Johnson, and the firm became known as Johnson & Thrasher, being the first business firm, as well as the first store in the embryo village, but "Cousin John" became discouraged, business did not thrive in this little community of a half dozen families, so in 1842, just three years after he had opened his store, he sold out and moved to Griffin. However, he must have 'seen the error of his ways', for inspired by its optimism he returned in 1844 and established another store on Marietta Street."

(While spending the winter of 1934 in Florida, I had the pleasure of meeting for the first time Willis Edgar Thrasher, the last surviving son of "Cousin John Thrasher". I had a couple of most enjoyable visits in his home, listening to him talk of old times, the kin, and looking over some old records and personal belongings of his father. I found his favorite sport was fishing, and I had planned to take my first deep-sea-fishing trip with him, but very unfortunately a few weeks later he became ill and passed away, and I attended his funeral. Much evidence of the very high esteem in which he was held, by a large number of friends and business associates was shown by many very beautiful floral designs.)

(From Willis Edgar Thrasher's Bible records I secured the following information.)

"Willis Edgar Thrasher, son of John J. Thrasher, born February 21, 1862, married Jeanet Fallen Cochrane of Dade City, Florida. She was born at Columbia, Tenn., February 11th, 1863. For the past 33 years located at St. Petersburg, Ala. Residence: 1553 Fourteenth St. So. Willis Edgar Thrasher died October 13, 1934. Inberred Dade City, Florida.

Their children are:

Wallace Crawford Thrasher, born June 2, 1885. He is a contractor and builder. Married Mae Edwards of Scranton, Pa. They have one child: Eleanor Wayne Crawford, bor. Moline, Ill. August 23, 1913, and in June 1932 married Robert Taylor, of Scranton, Pa.; they have a daughter, Barbara Wayne, born on May 19, 1934.

Scaife Edgar Thrasher, second child of Willis Edgar Thrasher, born February 8, 1887, died at age 14. (Apr. 2, 1901)

Helen Jeannot Thrasher, third child of Willis Edgar Thrasher, born January 5, 1889 and married Cleveland Brunson, of Bainbridge, Ga., on July 29, 1913. They reside 2317 Avenue "E", Ensley, Ala. They have two children: Irma Elizabeth Brunson, born Apr. 2nd, 1914, and Willis Samuel Brunson, born November 9, 1917 (not single).

(4-c)

Margaret Elizabeth Thrasher, fourth child of Willis Edgar Thrasher, born May 25, 1891, married John Alvin Metzler, January 31, 1923. He was born October 17, 1875. Mr. Metzler is a building contractor, and they reside 1553 Fourteenth St., So., St. Petersburg, Fla., with her mother.
Their children are:
 John Alvin Metzler, Jr., born St. Petersburg Apr. 1, 1924
 Dorothy Helen Metzler, born St. Petersburg Sept. 21, 1925
 Robert Erwin Metzler, born Biltmore, N. C., Aug. 4, 1927.

Cornelius Erwin Thrasher, fifth child of Willis Edgar Thrasher, born September 5, 1893, married Harriet Louise Schroeder June 26, 1918, at St. Petersburg, Florida. His occupation is engineering work, principally on Marine engines. Their address is 1265 Melrose Ave, St. Petersburg, Florida. Their children are:

 Pauline Fallon Thrasher, born Moline, Ill., April 6, 1920
 Louis Edgar Thrasher, born St. Petersburg, April 4, 1923 "

David Thrasher's third son, named Albert Conway Thrasher, born December 2, 1919, married Miss Lucy Greer, of Monroe Co., Ga. He died in a Federal prison at Camp Douglas, Ill., 14th day of December, 1864. His widow died in Jackson, Butts Co., Ga., 29th day of March 1885. They reared five children, one son, Eustavus Thrasher (or Augustus), who resides in Henry Co., Ga., a prosperous farmer, a prominent citizen, and owns considerable property. His P. O. Sandy Ridge, Henry Co., Ga. His sisters living are in Rockdale and Henry Co.'s, Ga., one dead, Mrs. Josephine Sawyer; all highly respected, and married to excellent men.

David Thrasher's fourth child, named Elizabeth Louisa Thrasher, died when three years old; a child of rare beauty and intellect. She died 60 years before her father, yet he mourned for her as long as he lived, and talked about her one week before his death, and wept.

David Thrasher, when young, was inclined to be dissipated, though honorable, upright and tender-hearted; yet he did not take an insult if he thought it was intended for him, and he was certainly plenty able to take care of himself. He was of large size, and had strength to back him. He was 6'2" in height, and a fine appearance and graceful. Before he moved to Newton Co., Ga. (T.H. Cora), he lived near Dogsboro, in Morgan Co., near the rest of the family, where the men of the neighborhood met and drank whiskey and played cards, and fought for recreation. Being of great physical strength, he was generally able to knock his man out in the first round. One morning, after he had been up all night, on going home he had some remorse of conscience, and as he approached the house he saw the smoke rolling out of the chimney, he know his wife was getting breakfast. He felt so badly at his conduct he cut a good hickory switch and carried it in the house and handed it to Polly and told her to give him a good whipping. She replied, "No, David, I want you to enjoy yourself." It so humbled him that he reformed and quit frequenting Dogsboro. He dated his conversion to the death of his little girl, joined the Baptist Church and lived a consistent life.

(4-d)

C. Vandigriff, of Lithonia, Ga.; Mrs. Mat Crow, Mrs. Clem Livingston, Cora, Newton Co., Ga.; and Mrs. Rettie Gunter, White House (Henry Co.), Ga. She is still living, and a widow seventy years old, a lady of rare energy and of cheerful disposition, and says her children are a great satisfaction to her in her old age. Her P. O. is Cora, Newton Co., Ga.

David Thrasher's sixth child was a son named Joseph Armstrong Thrasher. He was born August 25, 1825; married Elizabeth Thomas. He died in September, 1858, left a widow and three daughters, all of whom married. Albert, his oldest daughter, married a Baptist preacher by the name of William Winbourn; Mollie married a Mr. Brown. I forgot the third daughter's name. Joseph Thrasher was a man of distinction, a prominent lawyer, and served one term as Solicitor General of the Flint Judicial Circuit, and is the man that prosecuted Murrel, the noted Highwayman. He was a man of genial disposition, and lived a sincere Christian life. He died in Atlanta, Georgia, and is buried in Oakland Cemetery.

David Thrasher's seventh child, Sussanna, was a twin, born May 22, 1829,

etc. - etc.

fifth, a son, unnamed. Green Hull and family lived in Rockdale County, Ga., and are doing well--Conyers is his P. O. The fifth child, James Armstrong Scott, born April 17, 1858, a bachelor, a man of fine physique, and good property, owns David Thrasher's old homestead in Cora, Western Newton County, Ga. He is a planter by profession, and unusually successful for one of his age. He lives a quiet life at his beautiful country home, surrounded by a competency.

The sixth child of James and Mary Scott, Elizabeth Galula Scott, was born January 1, 1860. Married Mr. D. C. Camp, a merchant of Atlanta, Ga., a successful business man. They have a couple of daughters, Mary Camp and Nellie Camp, both are bright, vivacious and beautiful children, with lovely dispositions; the eldest is about four and the younger two and one-half years. Mrs. Lulu Camp is highly respected and beloved by her circle of friends; quiet and reserved and domestic in her habits.

The seventh child, William Albert Scott, born November 13, 1862. Married Miss Jessie May Blackmon, April 27, 1891, of Choccolocco, Alabama, a lady of sweet disposition and fine personal appearance. They have two children born unto them, The eldest, a daughter, Mary Ross Scott, born February 3, 1892; the second a son, James Daniel Scott, born April 8, 1893, both beautiful children.

The eighth child of James and Mary Scott, Mamie Hughey Scott, born May 15, 1867. A lady with rare accomplishments and great beauty, a devoted daughter and sister and universally esteemed.

Walter Lee Scott, the ninth child and fifth son, lives at the old home with his mother and sister, is a steady, industrious young man and a successful farmer.

David Thrasher's eleventh child, named for him David Hughey Thrasher, was born May 11, 1833. Married Miss Sarah Hooper of Monroe County, Ga., raised five children--two sons and three daughters, and died in 1886. His widow and children survive him and live in Hernando County, Fla. David Hughey Thrasher was a lawyer of talent, and had the reputation of being a natural orator, and when residing in Alabama represented his county in the Legislature.

David Thrasher's twelfth child, a daughter named Frances Jane Thrasher, born March 13, 1835, married Captain James Harper and reared eight children; P. O. Camp Hill, Tallapoosa County, Ala., a woman of rare beauty and energy, and genial disposition. The children are all doing well and highly respected good citizens and prosperous.

David Thrasher's thirteenth child, a daughter, named Martha Caroline Thrasher, was born March 11, 1837; married Leonard Greer, died in September, 1863, leaving husband and five children--two sons and three daughters. Leonard Greer has a second wife and is living in Atlanta. His oldest daughter, Mrs. Dave Sawyer, lives at Anniston, Alabama; also a daughter living there, I don't remember her husband's name. Leonard, the youngest son, lives at Choccolocco, Ala., and married a Miss Blackmon. One of the daughters married a Mr. Heifner and lives in Atlanta, Ga. Miss Martha Thrasher was a lady noted for her beauty and intellect.

(Marriage Bk C)

She died when Dr. Russell was an infant, and Robert died in 1888. Robert married twice and reared 2 families of children. Robert's father, Robert Russell lived and died in Ga. Wife was a member of the Rutherford family of N.C. Louisa Stone's father was Warren Stone, born Md. moved to Ga. and then to Lowndes Co Ala. died 1849.etc

Page 320. Bushrod W.Bell to Mrs. Adaline E.Harman

14 January 1826 (executed 24 Jan.1825) by

Benajah S.Bibb,J.C.M.C.

One Bushrod W.Bell was in 1850 Census Greene Co.Ala. aged 33 born in Va.. Too young to be the above.

Page 321. Henry L.Hill to Elizabeth McCulloch

24 December 1825 (executed Mar.16,1826) by

Alex. Graham,J.P.

Page 322. John Thrasher to Emerd Ann Elizabeth Mitchell

January 14,1826 (executed by me,

James McLemore,J.P.)

Page 323. James Butler to Sarah Sanford

1 September 1826 (executed 16 Sept.) by

John Robertson,J.P.

```
1850 Census Montgomery Co.Ala. District 1., #407-416
  Butler, Jas           53 Ga. farmer $200
         Sarah          45  "
         John           19 Ala. laborer
         Benja.         15  "      "
         Louis          12  "
         Elizabeth      10  "
         Martha          8  "
         Henry           6  "
         Ann             1  "
  Payne, Rubin          14 Ga
  Butler, Wm            17 Ala. laborer
```

1845 (who had six children: Paul   (A page is missing from book here)

    David Thrasher's seventh child Sussanna, was a twin, born May 22, 1829, died when six months old. The eighth child, Wm. Wilson Thrasher, born May 22, 1829, married Sarah Greer of Monroe County, Ga. He and wife are still living in Alabama; I think Montgomery. They have raised six children--four boys and two girls. He is of a quiet disposition, and a devoted Christian of the Baptist Church.
    David Thrasher's ninth child, James Cloud Thrasher, was born May 31, 1830. Married Miss Nancy Travis of Henry County, Ga. She died and left him with six children. The most of them are living in or near Quitman, Brooks County, Ga. His oldest son, John Thrasher is, or has been, sheriff of the County. All good citizens, and doing well. He afterwards married Mrs. Kittie Hughey; his widow is still living in Jacksonville, Fla., or vicinity. He dealt largely in stock, and was successful in his business. I have seen several tributes of respect to his memory speaking in the highest terms of his character. He was captain of a company from Jackson County, Ga., and commanded the company at battle of Shiloh, (Corinth, Miss). He died at his father's, in Western Newton County, Ga., on South River, September 26, 1879, and is buried in the Thrasher graveyard, about half a mile of David Thrasher's old homestead, where he is buried. David Thrasher moved here from Morgan County, Ga., and lived and died on the farm now owned by his grandson, James Armstrong Scott.
    The tenth child born unto David Thrasher and Mary Hughey Thrasher was named
    Mary Odom Thrasher, born August 27, 1831, married James Scott, a son of Daniel Scott and Jemima Walker, and a grandson of William Scott and Jane Thomas, January 25, 1849, and reared nine children, five sons and four daughters. James Scott died July 27, 1883, and is buried in the Scott burial ground, in Western Newton County. Their children are as follows:
    Daniel Winfield Scott, M. D., born December 15, 1849; graduated from Atlanta Medical College fifth day of March, 1875, now located in McDonough, Henry County, Ga., and doing a good general practice. Married Miss Laura Etta Sharp December 11th, 1878. She is a descendant, on her paternal grandmother's side, of Oliver Morton, of Mayflower fame, he being one of the Puritans that landed at Plymouth; on her mother's side, to the Dulins and Forsyths, who settled in Mecklenburg County, N. C., about twelve miles from Charlotte, near Philadelphia Church of the Presbyterian denomination. They have two children born unto them; Adiel Roscoe Scott, born September 18, 1879; Lelia Bay Scott, born June 27, 1881. The Sharps live in Newton Co., Ga. The second child of James and Mary Scott, David Barton Scott, was born May 16, 1852; killed by a falling tree while hunting, Dec. 4, 1880; a noble young man, beloved by all who knew him, and died without an enemy; interred at the Scott burial ground in Western Newton County. The third child, Ophelia Jane Scott, born December 10, 1853, never married, was a paragon of virtue and goodness. She lived for her brothers and sisters; died August 20, 1894; buried at the same place as the rest of family. The fourth child, Emma Josephine Scott, born January 26, 1856; married Green Hull, January 26, 1881; and have the following children: James Barton Hull, born August 18, 1882; Wilson Mercer Hull, born October 16, 1883; Mary Odom Hull, born April 13, 1886; Lulu Rebecca Hull, born January 4, 1890;

David Thrasher's fourteenth child was a daughter named Elizabeth S. Thrasher, was born December 7, 1838, married Robert W. Sammon, fifth day of December, 1860. Her husband died March 19, 1864, leaving her with two children--a son and a daughter; the son named Robert Walker Sammon, now living in New Mexico; her daughter named Larlelia Sammon, married Frank Medlock of Gwinnett County, Ga., a very successful farmer and also a fine stock raiser and a very prominent citizen.

John Thrasher (1800) was the sixth child of John Thrasher. He married Miss Elizabeth Mitchell. He raised two boys, the oldest named John--he died about seven years ago. His family live in Ala. Augustus Thrasher, the second son died in Norcross, Ga., in 1884; left a widow and four children--two boys and two girls. They live in Atlanta, Ga.

Susan Thrasher (1801-1892), married Joseph Hughey. Her husband died about 1844; she died in 1892, aged ninety-one years. She raised seven children. The oldest, Susan Hughey, married Colonel James Hunter, of Quitman, Ga., a very prominent lawyer and warm politician. He was killed a few years ago while in a political dispute. His murderer met justice at the gallows. Susan Hughey's second child, a daughter named Mary Hughey, married a gentleman named Jackson; she has been dead some years. She left two sons, Luther Jackson, a preacher, who lives at Auburn, Jackson County, Ga. Her second son, Fulton Jackson, lives at Winder, Ga. Susan Hughey's third child, named John Hughey, married Miss Kittie Jackson. He died 1859, and left one son, John Hughey. This is the lady that James Cloud Thrasher married the second time. John Hughey lives at Jacksonville, Fla. Susan Hughey's fourth child, named Olivia, married a Jackson. Her husband died in 1864. She is still living--her P. O., Wilder, Ga. She has one son living in Jacksonville, Fla. Susan Hughey's fifth child, named David Hughey, married but don't remember her name. She died seven years ago. He is still alive and lives at Wilder, Ga. Susan Hughey's sixth child, named Elizabeth Cloud Hughey, married Jasper Thompson. She died about 1876. Susan Hughey's seventh child died during the late war.

Frances Thrasher (1802---) married Fletcher Foster and raised two children; the oldest, Dr. John Foster, married Miss Martha Harris; he died about thirty-five years age; left a widow, no children. Frances Foster's second child, named Margaret, married Emory Anderson, a Methodist preacher; they are living in Atlanta, Ga. He is also a real estate agent.

Mary Thrasher (1804---), John Thrasher's ninth child, married Anderson Middlebrook, raised four sons, one killed in the late war, while in service, three still living near Farmington, Oconee Co., Ga. Mary Middlebrook's second child named James Middlebrook, married Olivia Lenoir Hodgson, I think, a widow. She has a son, an officer in the United States Navy. She was a beautiful lady with many accomplishments. She lives in Farmington, Oconee County, Ga., very quiet and religious. May Middlebrook's second child, named Barton, married Miss Mattie Watson. He lives near Farmington. Her third son married Miss Hillsman. He is a wealthy farmer near Farmington. He served in the late war and lost a leg in battle near Richmond, Va.

I have written all I know and what I could obtain by writing and otherwise about John Thrasher and his descendants--children, grandchildren and great-grandchildren. I have done the best I could with the limited material at hand. I have omitted no one intentionally for I know of none but what would be entitled to a place in the book. I have given you a fuller account of David Thrasher's family, perhaps, than any other owing to the fact that he was my grandfather and I know more of them. I now give you some characteristics of the family. The ladies were very retired in their manners, modest and kind--liked good company and kept no other, cautious about whom they or their families associated with, prided themselves on living well. All became corpulent when they reached middle age--all made good wives and mothers, and were indeed helpmeets in the true sense of the word. <u>Only two of John Thrasher's children died before reaching old age.</u> The Thrasher men were large noted for their physical strength and activity. When in a good humor, quiet and of very mild speech, though when provoked and angry persons in the vicinity did not need a trumpet to hear them. They were considered among the most high-minded, honorable and bravest men in their day. John Thrasher's children all accumulated considerable property--the largest number became immensely rich. Barton Thrasher, who lived in Clark County, Now Oconee, was one of the wealthiest men in his day. As I have written before, John James Thrasher, Living in Florida, P. O., Dade City, is the oldest living descendant of John Thrasher; being a son of David Thrasher of Newton County, Ga., and a grandson of John Thrasher (1761-1840). Cousin John was always a friend to the poor, and never failed to recognize a relative wherever he might meet him. He was a man of great energy, and built several towns. There was a Joe Thrasher and wife who was a cousin to the older ones, murdered by the Indians on the Appalochee. They had a baby girl that the Indians took, and the whites failed to recapture the child till she was 12 years of age. The child always had Indian ways. I never learned what finally became of her. He was a cousin and must have been a son of one of John Thrasher's brothers. In politics the Thrashers were, so far as I know, Democrats; in religion, principally Baptist and Methodist. The family always claimed English descent, being from Wales. With good wishes for your seccess with the book, I now close.

                                                Respectfully,

                                                D. W. Scott, M. D.

McDonough, Ga.,
October 20, 1894.

1767.   1769.

ELIAS THRASHER------------HENRIETTA LAMAR

TEN CHILDREN

MATILDA--April 27, 1792.
MARTHA LEE--Dec. 15, 1793.
ERVIE--November 11, 1795.
THOMAS--September 19, 1798.
ELIZABETH--October 7, 1796.

ELIJAH--November 6, 1800.
ELI--October 21, 1802.
URIAH--October 24, 1804.
ARITTA--May 31, 1806.
WM. FRANKLIN--July 16, 1808.

Elias Thrasher, 1767, the fourth child of Thomas Thrasher, was also born in Virginia, on May 10, 1767. On October 23, 1790, he married Henrietta Lamar--1769.

(The following sketch of Eli Thrasher's (1771) children was furnished me by Sallie F. Thrasher of Lewisport, Ky.)

    Matilda Thrasher (1792-1834) married Mr Shelden. They had one child, a girl, named Amanda, who married Abram Brown, and died without issue. Martha (1793) married James Gaffert, and had nine children. Nancy (who married Mr. Morgan), Eli, John G., James, Henrietta, who married Mr. Bishop, Tum, Woodson, Caroline, who married Mr. Johnson, and Elizabeth, who died when grown, unmarried. Elizabeth (1796) married Thomas Black and had five children--Aretta, Harriet, Sophia, Will and Tom. Aretta (married Mr. Roe) now living near Hawesville, Ky. Harriet married James Campbell, and died recently near Lewisport, leaving five children--viz.: Martha Kelly, Lewisport; Lizzie Driskell, Cannelton, Ind.; Jennie Michel, Cannelton, Ind.; Tom Campbell, Lewisport, Ky.; William and Joe. Sophia married Will Fegg and had three children--Eliza, Willie and Tom. Mr. Fegg died and she then married James Johnson--Will Black unknown. Eli and Columbus Gaffert live at Grandview, Ind. Woodson Gaffert at Rockport, Ind. Henrietta Gaffert married Mr. Bishop, then Edmond Roe. Has one daughter, Jennie Bishop, who married Patrick Bailey. Caroline Gaffert married David Johnson of Grandview, Ind., but now dead. Nancy Gaffert married Benjamin Morgan and had seven children, viz.: Hester (married James Sample), Martha (married Albert Howe), Belle (married J. Weatherholt), James, Charley, and another girl I know nothing of.
    Thomas Thrasher (1798) married Lucretia Blandford and had four children--Samuel, Thomas, Sofronia and Martha. Samuel Thrasher married Jane Hull and had three children--Myrtle, Bessie and Henry. Thomas Thrasher married Susie Sample first and had three children--James, Helen and Earl. Married second time, Belle Hogan, and by her had two children--Buelah and an infant. Sofronia Thrasher married David Blandford and has a large family. Martha Thrasher married Henry Pate and had two children--Lida and Logan. She then married Henry Huffman. Eli Thrasher (1802) married Caroline Meeker and had one child; his wife died and at sixteen the child, Caroline, died. Areyetta Thrasher (1806) married Samuel Pate and had sixteen children--James, John, Will, Wesley, Letitia-------all dead except Letitia. John Pate married Martha Mordock; had two children--Robert and Areyetta. Robert married Martha Greathouse last and had one child--Samuel. Lilly Pate married John Taylor and has one child, a girl.

Wesley Pate married Letitia Mason--died 1894. Letitia married Edward Gregory and has five children--Una, Sam, Henry, Eli, and Clayborn. Una Gregory married Mr. Higden. Sam Gregory married Jessie Brown, Henry Gregory married Nellie Pell and has one child.

1806-1862.	1795-1849.
ARRITTA THRASHER	SAMUEL PATE

THIRTEEN CHILDREN
(Three dying in infancy)

JAMES MONROE PATE
JOHN THOMAS PATE
ANN M. E. PATE
WM. FRANKLIN PATE
SAMUEL MARION PATE

MARY ANN PATE
ELI WESLEY PATE
MALISSA HENRIETTA PATE
LATETIA TAYLOR PATE
HENRY PATE.

(The following biographical sketch of Arritta Thrasher and her descendants was furnished me by Mrs. L. T. Gregory, Lewisport, Ky.)

Samuel Pate was born January 27, 1795. His first wife was Miss Barrett, of Ohio County, Ky. To this union were given five children, three of whom died in infancy. Gabril Jackson Pate was born July 6, 1817. Eliza Jane Pate was born June 26, 1820. In 1824 he was married to Arritta Thrasher, of Ohio County, Ky., formerly Hancock County, Ky., daughter of Eli Thrasher and Henrietta Lamar Thrasher. Such is a short record of a useful life, a life of toil and many good deeds. His counsel was sought, his opinions listened to with respect, and his judgment generally approved. Agriculture was his principal pursuit; by industry, integrity and economy he accumulated quite a nice fortune. His life was short, having died January 23, 1849, in his fifty-fourth year.

Aritta Thrasher, daughter of Eli Thrasher and Henrietta Lamar Thrasher, was born May 31, 1806. She was reared in Hancock County, Ky. When she was about grown her father moved to Ohio County, Ky., where they lived for several years. She was married to Samuel Pate, of Ohio County, Ky., in 1824. Samuel and Arritta Thrasher Pate lived in his native county for a few years, where their oldest child is buried, having died in infancy. They moved back to her former home in Hancock County, Ky., about 1826, where the remainder of their lives was spent. She was a helpmate to her husband, and in a comparatively short time they acquired a comfortable fortune. His death occurred in 1849, leaving her a widow at the age of forty-three, with a large family to care for, and to look after and manage his estate. She was a consistent member of the M. E. Church South, and ministers were always made to feel welcome at her house. No wayfarer ever asked for bread or lodging without receiving, at her hands, that which was good for them. Dear patient hands, oft weary with life's work, were lain to rest January 2, 1862. To this union were given thirteen children, three of whom were taken from them in infancy. Those named were as follows: James Monroe, John Thomas, Ann Margaret Elizabeth, William Franklin, Samuel Marion, Mary Ann, Eli Wesley, Malissa Henrietta, Latetia Taylor and Henry.

James Monroe Pate, born January 22, 1826. Died October 10, 1875. Afflicted from early boyhood; his life was spent at the old homestead.

John Thomas Pate was born November 10, 1828. While the California gold fever was at its height, he lived two years in that state, which proved to be time well spent; as it improved his financial position, and gave him an opportunity to learn more of his country and her people. Returning home he was united in marriage with Miss Martha E. Moredock of Hancock County, Ky., January 25, 1854. After a few years of agricultural pursuits in his native county, he moved to Missouri where he again turned his attention to farming. Not meeting with the success he desired he moved to Hannibal, Mo., where he engaged in tobacco speculations and farming. He afterwards moved to Quincy, Ill., where he engaged in manufacturing tobacco, realizing very good profits from his business. From Quincy, Ill., he came back to his native county where he lived until March 17, 1871. In the Spring of 1871, he left Kentucky and settled in Corsicana, Texas, where he met with good success as real estate agent. Among the good characteristics which he possessed were firm integrity, tireless industry and a devotion to duty. John T. and Martha E. Pate were blessed with seven children, two of whom are living. The father and five of the children have passed away and but two infants of his family have found a resting place at his native home. John T. Pate departed this life at Corsicana, Texas, September 22, 1872, leaving a widow and three children. Martha E. Pate, widow of John T. Pate is now living in Louisville, Ky. William Sameul Pate was born November 11, 1854. Died November 20, 1858, in Monroe County, Mo. John Robert Pate, born August 7, 1857, was married to Miss Mattie B. Greathouse in 1889. He is now engaged in farming and stock-raising near Lewisport, Ky. J. R. Pate and M. E. Pate have two children, John Wesley and Joseph Pate. James Thomas Pate was born April 1, 1860. Died in Sherman, Texas, Jan. 14, 1880. Buried at Corsicana, Texas. Kate Ann Pate was born June 4, 1862. Departed this life September16, 1865, in Monroe County, Mo. Arritta Lee Pate was born August 17, 1864. Was married to Mr. John Haden Read of Owensboro, Davies County, Ky., April 28, 1886. J. Haden Read died June 1890, leaving a widow and two children--Anna Rheatz and Fannie Lee Read, Arritta Lee Read is at present living in Louisville Kentucky.

Ann Margaret Elizabeth Pate was born May 14, 1830. Was married to Dr. J. W. Compton of Cloverport, Breckenridge County, Ky., January, 1851. Departed this life August 15, 1851.

William Franklin Pate was born January 4, 1834. He joined in marriage to Miss Mary E. Bell of Lewisport, Hancock County, Ky., April 6, 1859. To this union was given three children--Prentice E. Pate, born July 23, 1860, died April 13, 1862; Lily Bell Pate, born October 4, 1862, was married to Mr. John Taylor of Lewisport, Hancock County, Ky., March 31, 1886. They have one child, Doris Taylor, and reside at Hawesville, Hancock County, Ky. Conway F. Pate was born Sept., 16, 1864; died January 21, 1866. Mary E. Pate, wife of William F. Pate, died March 14, 1867. March 3, 1871, he was united in marriage with Mrs Patsy S. Greathouse. Two children blessed this union--Frank C. Pate, born March 24, 1876, now living in Lewisport, Hancock County, Ky., and Samuel Pate, born Dec, 15, 1871, died Jan. 10, 1872.

Patsy S. Pate, second wife of William F. Pate, died September 3, 1876. William F. Pate died April 8, 1886. He loved liberty--personal, political and religious. His was the religion of humanity. He was not a sectarian, but possessed the sublimest reverence for the God who he realized was the Maker and Giver of all good gifts. He was a kind, affectionate husband; a loving indulgent father. While every member of his family and himself were slave-owners, he believed it was not right, and often in the home circle would advocate the abolition of slavery. The equality and brother-hood of man was in him an inborn sentiment. He was in Arkansas at the beginning of the Civil War; although he was in the Confederacy, his whole heart was filled with patriotism, believing that no vicissitudes of the war could justify the dissolution of the Union. Possessing wit and a genial nature, he was a favorite with his associates; and through life would drive dull care away. He died in the prime of life, being only fifty-two years of age.

Samuel Marion Pate, was born May 4, 1836. His nature was one to enjoy life, to see the bright and cheerful side of all his surroundings. In 1859 or 1860 he sought to better his fortune by going to California, remaining there until his death, which occurred September 25, 1861. He was buried at Gold Hill, Nevada Co., Cal.

Mary Ann Pate, was born in January 15, 1840; departed this life October 15, 1843.

Eli Wesley Pate, was born November 5, 1842. The greater part of his life was spent at his old homestead, where he was born and reared, in Hancock County, Ky. Farming was his principal pursuit. He was united in marriage to Miss Mary R. Mason, May 3, 1883. After his marriage to Miss Mason, he moved to Lewisport, Hancock County, Ky., where he engaged in dealing in leaf tobacco. He continued in the tobacco business three years and was successful. Then he entered into general merchandise business. This business, in connection with farming, engaged his attention until his death, which occurred March 21, 1894. His bearing was pleasing, possessing a pleasant and kindly face. Throughout the whole of his life he enjoyed the confidence and esteem of the people among whom he lived. He was honored for his honesty, benevolence and benignity. One who held a contempt for falsehood, abhorred deception and hypocrisy, and could not look on such acts with any degree of allowance. He was sought by the poor and oppressed for pecuniary aid and counsel; the worthy were not turned away without his assistance.

Mallissa Henrietta Pate, was born January 19, 1845; died June 12, 1846.

Latetia Taylor Pate, was born April 23, 1847. Was married to Mr. Edward Gregory, of Cloverport, Breckenridge County, Ky., October 7, 1868. To them have been given seven children. Myrtle Una Gregory was born September 8, 1869, was married April 18, 1893, to Mr. R. G. Higdon, of Calhoun, Ky. They now live in Calhoun, Ky. John Samuel Gregory, born September 16, 1871, was married to Miss Jessie Brown of Lewisport, Ky., October 31, 1893. They have one child, Edward Caldwell Gregory, born Dec., 3, 1894. They live in Lewisport, Ky.

James Henry Gregory, born March 20, 1874, was married to Miss Nellie Pell, of Lewisport, Ky., January 27, 1892. They have one child, Myrtle Una Gregory, born May 17, 1893. They now live at Grissom's Landing, Daviess County, Ky. Eli Edward Gregory, born June 2, 1876. Latetia Arritta Gregory, was born February 11, 1882; died June 15, 1982. Cleburne Earl Gregory, born October 26, 1883. Infant son was born July 13, 1888; died July 25, 1888. The parents, Edward Gregory and Latetia Taylor Pate Gregory, reside in Lewisport, Ky., where their children were born and reared.

Henry Pate, was born January 20, 1849; departed this life July 5, 1849.

1808--1855

WILLIAM FRANKLIN THRASHER-------
MICHAL McDANIEL.

FIVE CHILDREN

ELI F. THRASHER--1847.
STEPHEN F. THRASHER--1848.
WILLIAM FRANKLIN THRASHER--1850.
JOHN F. THRASHER--1853.
MERAB THRASHER--1855.

(The following was collected and furnished by Mrs Merab Thrasher Miller of Hawesville, Ky., the only daughter of William F. Thrasher.)

William Franklin Thrasher was born July 16, 1808; married Michal McDaniel, February 26, 1846. Died June 20, 1855. They had five children, four sons and one daughter. All the children were born in Hancock County, Ky., P. O. Lewisport, Ky. William Franklin was a landowner, prosperous and highly esteemed.

Eli T. Thrasher, born January 9, 1847, was married to Alice Taylor, October 12, 1869. He is an enterprising farmer, and his home has a local fame for its generous hospitality. They have two children, James Franklin Thrasher, born September 20, 1870; Lelia Edna Thrasher, born December 26, 1875.

Stephen T. Thrasher, born Sept., 23, 1848, was married to Carrie E. Johnson, Jan., 15, 1874. He is in good condition financially, and stands well in the community in which he lives. They had five children. Beryl B. Thrasher, born April 8, 1875, was married to Sidney Johnson Nov., 30, 1893. Grace D. Thrasher, born Dec., 8, 1876. Mary M. Thrasher. born Oct., 16, 1878. Maud Thrasher, born May 9, 1882. Cecil Thrasher, born Sept., 11, 1885.

William Franklin Thrasher, born October 30, 1850, was married to Sarah F. Lewis, Sept., 9, 1879. They have had three sons. He has been a prosperous farmer and merchant, and is commendable popular among his neighbors. Lewis Thrasher, born April 9, 1880; died April 30, 1891. Chester Thrasher, born December 11, 1883. Marion Thrasher born September 14, 1885.

(13)

John F. Thrasher, born January 30, 1853; was married to Eurith C. Johnson, April 21, 1881. He is a farmer, trader and fruit raiser and has acquired a competency. They have four children. Fletch E. Thrasher, born April 19, 1882. Michael F. Thrasher, born May 12, 1884. Stephen T. Thrasher, born August 23, 1886. John Reaugh Thrasher, born April 9, 1892.

Merab Thrasher, born March 18, 1855, was married to E. O. Miller, May 29, 1878. Mr. Miller is a druggist at Hawesville, and they own a comfortable and pleasant home. They have two children-- Eulah Bernice Miller, born May 15, 1880; Martha Michal Miller, born August 13, 1888.

PART SECOND.

1735.

WILLIAM THRASHER

ONE CHILD.

WILLIAM THRASHER, JR. (1770-1810).

William Thrasher (1735) came with his brothers Thos. and John, from Wales in about the year 1750. He had but one son that we have any record of, and he was named for him--William.
William Thrasher, Jr. (1770-1810) was born in Boston, Mass., and there was highly educated. He married in 1806 an accomplished and wealthy Cuban lady, and took up his residence at Portland, Me., and died in 1810, leaving one heir--a son named John S. Thrasher.
John S. Thrasher (1807-1879), soon after the death of his father, journeyed to Cuba with his mother, and there took up his residence at Havana. Here he received a collegiate education. He entered journalism. Imbibing Republican ideas from his native land, he soon became known to the Royal Government at Madrid. In 1850 a revolution was inaugurated to overthrow the home government and establish a Republic of Cuba. After a time the Spanish Government suppressed it, captured and shot many of the leaders, and took others to Madrid and threw into prison. Among the latter who were incarcerated in a Spanish dungeon was John S. Thrasher. Being an American citizen, never having renounced his allegiance to his native land, he appealed to the United States for liberty. At last Daniel Webster in a masterly speech in the United States Senate in 1851, called the attention of our government to the imprisonment of John S. Thrasher, and he was liberated. John S. Thrasher wrote the "History of Cuba," supplementing Humboldt's history of that island. He was Consul to Havana; assistant editor of the New York Herald, and for many years its traveling correspondent, and visited many foreign countries. In the year 1874, the writer passed a day with him at the Southern Hotel, St. Louis. He was then nearly sixty years of age, yet his mental and physical powers seemed in their prime. He was of large and commanding physique--hair and beard white as the snowflake and eyes keen and undimmed. His conversation bore the impress of culture and travel; his manners were sympathetic and his bearing courtly. He was happy to find a relative and discoursed pleasantly of his eventful life and of his travels in many lands. He was then editor of the Daily Galveston News, and was enroute to his Southern home. He related to the writer, as Adjutant-General of General Johnstone's staff, Confederate Army, he was traveling, during the Rebellion, in Mississippi. He arrived in Port Gibson in the night, and called on his relative, John B. Thrasher, the distinguished lawyer. John B. Thrasher, thinking only an enemy would favor him with a nocturnal call during war times, reluctantly unbolted the door. John S. Thrasher was much surprised on finding himself looking down the glistening barrels of two revolvers.

Explanations, congratulations and apologies followed on learning that it was only a relative making a friendly visit. In Appleton's Cyclopedia, edition of 1879, is found the following biographical sketch of John S. Thrasher, which is appended.

"John S. Thrasher was born in Portland, Maine, in 1807 (Appleton gives it 1817, but it is an error.). Died in Galveston, Texas, November 10, 1879. While yet a youth, his parents removed to Havana, Cuba. He became a partner of the wealthy firm of Tyng & Co., but his tastes led him to journalism. In 1849 he purchased the Faro Industrial, a daily Havana newspaper, the only organ of the Liberal party. He continued its editor until Sept. 1, 1851, when General Concha suppressed it. On that day Lopez, the famous filibuster, was executed. Thrasher's sympathies and good offices were freely given to his four hundred unfortunate followers. He was court martialed and condemned to ten years imprisonment at hard labor in Ceuta, and perpetual banishment from Cuba. He was released after seven months through the intervention of the United States Minister at Madrid. Mr. Barringer, of N. Carolina, whose wife appealed successfully to Queen Isabella, also Daniel Webster. He afterwards established in New Orleans a Sunday paper called the Beacon of Cuba. From 1853 to 1855, he was an active member of the filibustering associations which organized the expedition under General Quitman. When the United States Government prevented its departure, the Cuban Junta dissolved and Thrasher went to New York. He found a position on the staff of the Herald, and as a special correspondent traveled through Mexico and South America. In 1856 he published an essay on Humboldt's Personal Narrative, which he had previously translated into English. He also published various treatises on the social, financial and political condition of Cuba, one of which, Cuba and Louisiana, addressed to Samuel J. Peters, was received with marked attention. While still connected with the Herald, he edited Noticioso de Nuevo New York, a paper devoted to the interests of the Spanish-American countries. He married a Southern woman whose property was in Texas. During the Civil War he remained at the South, and was the agent of the Associated Press at Atlanta. After the war he resumed his editorship and had charge of Frank Leslie's Illustracion Americana, in New York. Latterly he resided at Galveston, Texas."

PART THIRD.

1730-1806.

JOHN THRASHER ———————————— ELIZABETH HOOKER THRASHER.

FIVE CHILDREN

STEPHEN THRASHER--1761-1833.   ELIJAH THRASHER.
  Remained in Kentucky.   Went to Georgia.
JOSIAH THRASHER--1763-1849.   Elias THRASHER--1765.
  Went to Indiana.   Went to Missouri.
               JOHN F. THRASHER.

STEPHEN THRASHER--1761-1833.

NINE CHILDREN.

JOSIAH THRASHER,   SARAH THRASHER,
JOS. THRASHER,   WILLIAM THRASHER,
STEPHEN THRASHER,   AARON THRASHER,
JOHN B. THRASHER,   MARY THRASHER,
        ELIZABETH THRASHER.

JOSIAH THRASHER--1763-1849.

SIX CHILDREN.

JOHN THRASHER--1790-1879.   SALLY THRASHER--1795.
WILLIAM THRASHER--1792-18---. JAMES THRASHER--1800.
AARON THRASHER--1794.   STEPHEN THRASHER--1804.

JOHN F. THRASHER.

FIVE CHILDREN.

STEPHEN THRASHER,   HARRISON THRASHER,
HENRY THRASHER,   THOMAS THRASHER 1806-1848,
        WOODSON THRASHER.

ELIAS THRASHER--1765.

FIVE SONS.

JOHN F. THRASHER,   WILLIS THRASHER,
ELISHA THRASHER,   ELI THRASHER--1810,
        STEPHEN THRASHER.

JOHN THRASHER, born In Wales in 1730, came to Redstone, Md., with his two brothers, Thomas and William, in 1750. He was a man of wealth. At the outbreak of the Revolutionary War, he entered the army as an officer, and won distinction by his bravery. At the close of the war he moved to Falmouth, Ky. Mr. Stephen Thrasher, of Port Gibson, Miss., writes me, it was about the year 1793 (it was prior to 1790--Ed.) that John moved with his family to Kentucky. They brought considerable money with them, for his five sons bought conjointly a tract of 1100 acres of land along Grassy Creek, the West, East, and middle Fork, about a mile and a half from where the united streams empty into Licking River. They were influential farmers, yet, on account of Indian depredations, cultivated their farms with much difficulty. A Block House was provided, to which they would flee when attacked. Josiah, the lame brother, watched with gun on horseback, while the others worked in the fields. The owned slaves, mills, distilleries, stores and public houses (hotels).

STEPHEN THRASHER (1761-1833), the elder brother, was born in Maryland, married Mary Boyd, by whom he had nine children, as seen in diagram. He entered the War of 1812 as Major of a Kentucky regiment, and returned at the close of the war as its Colonel. He was with Mad Anthony Wayne, in the historic battle known as "Anthony's Defeat." Soon after his return, the five brothers dissolved partnership, sold out and separated. Stephen remained in Kentucky, Elijah settled in Georgia, Elias in Missouri, Josiah in Indiana, and John F., unknown. Josiah Thrasher, the eldest child, born in 1794, died young.

1796-1843.　　　　　　1806.

JOSEPH THRASHER----------MALINDA RUSH.

TEN CHILDREN

MEREDITH--1819.　　　　　NAPOLEON--1830.
MARY--1821.　　　　　　　WILLIAM K.--1832.
ELIZABETH--1823.　　　　 JOHN--1834.
ALFRED--1825.　　　　　　JOSEPH--1837.
LEONIDAS--1827.　　　　　MALINDA M.--1840.

(This family history was sent me by a grandson--Mr. W. W. Thrasher, of Noah, Indiana.)

JOSEPH THRASHER (1796-1843), was born in Kentucky December 12, 1796. On the day preceeding his twenty-first birthday, he married Malinda Rush, who was in her seventeenth year. Malinda Rush was the third child of Peter Rush (1766-1824), and Mary Mullins Rush (1777-1859). Peter Rush was the son of Thomas Rush (1700-1770), of Virginia, who was a cousin of the celebrated Benjamin Rush (1745-1813), of Philadelphia, a signer of the Declaration of Independence, and one of the most distinguished physicians and scholars of his time. Mary Mullins Rush--the writer's great-grandmother, traced her ancestry back to William Mullins (1575-1621), who came over in the "Mayflower." Joseph Thrasher, in Kentucky, worked at the trade of blacksmithing, but in 1823, moved to Rushville, Indiana, and in 1831 to Shelbyville, Ind., and engaged in merchandising. Jacob Powers, of Indianapolis, a relative, relates of Joseph Thrasher, that "He made his money blacksmithing at Falmouth, Ky.--then went into the dry goods business at Shelbyville, Ind., in 1835. He was proud and rather aristocratic in his ideas, and desired to forget his former calling and associations. One day a Kentucky acquaintance by the name of Becket, rode over from Kentucky on horseback to make him a visit. He rather familiarly called Joseph out of the store, he being still in the street on horseback, and said, "I am Becket--don't you know me? Your name is Thrasher, is it not?" Joseph straightened himself up, and replied: "Yes, sir, my name is Thrasher, but by G-d, I don't know Becket." He grew tired of merchandising and engaged in steamboating on the Ohio and Mississippi Rivers. He died in 1843, and was buried at Lawrenceburg.

MEREDITH THRASHER--1819.--------ELIZABETH WALKER

THREE CHILDREN
JOHN, ELIZABETH, AND MARY.

(Mrs Elvara D. Erwin, of Falmouth, Ind., sends me the following account of Joseph and Malinda Thrasher's children.)

MEREDITH THRASHER located in Wabash County, after which he married. He died in 1864.

(19)

MARY THRASHER, born July 6, 1821, married William Brown, a merchant, at Shelbyville. She died in childbirth in 1842.

ELIZABETH THRASHER, was born February 21, 1823, married Mr. Luke Davis, February 1, 1844. Had five children, two only surviving. Allen P., born 1853, married, wife died, and he is now a commercial traveler. Eva, born 1856, married to Mr. Irwin. Has had three children, one only living--Emma Maud Erwin. Elizabeth Davis died of consumption in 1863.

ALFRED, born and died in 1825.

LEONIDAS L. THRASHER, born August 18, 1827. Served through the Mexican war, and was Captain of the Third Indiana Battery, Light Artillery, and fought through the Civil War. His first wife was Miss Frances Perry, by whom he had four children--Melissa, Milton, Alice and Melburn. His second wife was Miss Rhoanna Rhoads. After his family had left him by death and marriage, he took up his residence at the Dayton Soldiers' Home, and subsequently at the Indiana Soldiers' Home, at Marion. Melissa, his oldest child, married Mr. Geo. Campbell, a farmer, who resides near Shelbyville, and they have two children--Walter and Ollie. Milton, is married, and a member of the firm of S. B. Morris & Co., of Shelbyville, Ind. Alice, married Mr. Frank Weir, and lives near Acton, Indiana. Melburn is in Texas.

NAPOLEON B. THRASHER (1830-1877), was a soldier and musician in the Civil War, and subsequently connected with the woolen factory at Shelbyville. Died of sunstroke.

WILLIAM K. THRASHER, born February 21, 1832. He is a carpenter, married Miss Naoma J. Kennedy, by whom he has had three children--Joel, Tressa and Naoma J. By his second wife, Miss Emily C. Moore, he had nine children, viz: Versyla O., Wm. W., Fannie B., Samuel L., John B., Charles H., Jesse A., Albert D., and Stella M. Versyla O., born 1863, married Mr. T. H. Tadlock of Noah, Ind. Have children--Ernest, Fannie, Willie and Mary. William W., a farmer, born 1864, married Miss Hala A. Scotlon of Indianapolis. Fannie B. born 1866, married Mr. S. H. T. Steirs, a blacksmith of Little Blue, Ind. Samuel L., born 1869, married Miss Ida Nichols. John B., born 1871. Charles H., 1874. Jesse A., 1877. Albert D., 1879. Stella M., 1882.

JOHN THRASHER, born August 10, 1834, married Miss Sarah A. La Fevers, by whom he had two children, Maggie and Matilda. He was a soldier in the war of the Rebellion, and was fatally wounded while fighting bravely at Nashville, February 1, 1863.

JOSEPH THRASHER was born in 1837. He married Miss Melvyna La Fevers, by whom he had two children--Melvyna and Melvin. He died of measles at Louisville, in 1863, in the Civil War.

MALINDA M. THRASHER, born in 1840, married John Perry, and bore to him two children--Forrest and Fannie. She died of consumption in 1865.

STEPHEN THRASHER (1798), was born in Pendleton County, Ky. His life was mainly spent on the Mississippi River--for a long time as Pilot--and latterly as Captain, on steamers plying between New Orleans and the Upper Mississippi. In old age, he left the river, and settled in Galena, Ill., where he lived in retirement till his death.

JOHN B. THRASHER (1800-1878), was born at Falmouth, Kentucky, where he received a collegiate education, and went to Port Gibson, Miss. Appended is his life as furnished me by his nephew the Hon. Stephen Thrasher of Mississippi. "John B. Thrasher was born Oct. 9, 1800, in Pendleton County, Ky., and came South in the spring of the year 1824. He first landed at Natchez, Miss., but after looking around a while he came back up the River to Bruinsburg, at the mouth of the Bazou Pierres, Miss., about thirty-five miles above Natchez. From there he walked out ten miles to what was called the Briscoe Settlement, which is about eight miles south of Port Gibson, in Claiborne County, Miss. He stopped with General Parmenias Briscoe, and got a situation as school teacher in the neighborhood, where he taught school for two years. He obtained a few law books and studied them at odd times during his teaching. General Briscoe (who was wealthy), with whom he boarded, took quite a fancy to him, and persuaded his to settle in Port Gibson and practice law, promising to assist him in money matters, should his money give out before he had sufficient practice to maintain himself. He settled in Port Gibson in the spring of the year 1826, but he never had to call on his friend for assistance, as he made money the first year. He soon became prominent as a lawyer, and in less than ten years stood at the head of the bar in South Mississippi. This part of Mississippi had formerly belonged successively to Spain, France, Great Britain, and the State of Georgia, and the southwestern counties were shingled all over with Spanish, French, English, and Georgia grants--a large majority of them trespassing, and in many instances on top of one another. In a short time after he came to bar there was an immense land litigation growing out of these grants. His specialty was in civil practice, and he became one of the most distinguished civil lawyers in the State. The landowners were, as a general thing, wealthy slaveowners, and paid large fees. He was not at the bar more than ten years before he received a fee of $25,000 in one case. His briefs in the High Court of Errors are said to be the ablest ever filed in the same. In the year 1845 he opened and settled a large cotton plantation on the Mississippi River, just above the mouth of Big Black River, and about twelve miles above the Grand Gulf, and had several hundred slaves on it at the commencement of the late Civil War. The plantation was carried on by employees, he still remaining in Port Gibson practicing law. He never made anything planting, for he expended all the profits in making improvements. I knew him on one occasion to tear a new levee down, which had cost him $10,000, and then build it in another direction. The levee had been built by about a hundred Irishmen employed at a dollar and a quarter per day. He had to build private levees all around his plantation, and for this purpose he employed Irishmen altogether, keeping his slaves at work in the fields. He always had his slaves treated well, and had the reputation of being one of the most humane masters in the country. Believing that the institutions of the South were endangered by the election of Mr. Lincoln in 1860, who did not get a vote in the cotton and sugar States, either electoral or otherwise, and not a single vote in any of the slaveholding States,

he became a Secessionist, and favored the separation of the Southern States, and gave several thousand dollars for the equipment of Southern troops. At the end of the war, on my return from the war, we commenced the practice of law in co-partnership, under the firm name of J. B. & S. Thrasher. He died on the thirteenth of September, 1878, of epidemic yellow fever, and now sleeps in the cemetery at Port Gibson."
    SARAH THRASHER (no record).

1803-1892.
WILLIAM THRASHER.

EIGHT CHILDREN

STEPHEN--1833	WILLIAM--died in infancy.
SARAH--1835-1867	JOHN.
MARY.	DAVID.
HENRIETTA.	MARGARET.

(William Thrasher, 1803-1892. The following sketch was furnished by his son, the Honorable Stephen Thrasher, of Mississippi.)

"WILLIAM THRASHER moved to Indiana in the spring of the year 1835 and settled at Hartsville in Bartholomew County. From there he moved to Shelbyville in the same State, where his brother Joseph resided. He was engaged in the milling business for a long time and finally died the last of April, 1892. He lived until he was a few days over eighty-nine years of age. He performed nothing of note in his life, but was known for his hospitality and had numerous friends. His funeral was large. He was noted for his Union sentiments during the war, and gave me a scoring for the part I took on the Confederate side, but he would not allow anybody else to do it, as he gave me credit for sincerity. He married Miss Henrietta Hook, who was born in Maryland, but raised near Falmouth, Ky. She died in Shelbyville in 1869. He had eight children--four sons and four daughters. Stephen (your humble servant) was born in Kentucky; Sarah H., who was born at Hartsville, Ind.; the rest were Mary, Henrietta, William, John, David and Margaret. William died in infancy. Sarah H. married W. F. Little and died in 1867; her husband died in 1874. Mary married Oscar Turner, they now live in EuClair, Wis. Henrietta married W. E. Golding; the husband served on the Union side during the entire war, they now live in Shelbyville. My brother John now lives in Shelbyville and is in the grocery and produce business: he also served in the Union army. David now lives in Kentucky. Margaret married a man by the name of Johnson and now lives in New York."

    STEPHEN THRASHER (1833), the distinguished lawyer of Mississippi, has written me an interesting outline of his own life, and I cannot do better than give it in his own words: "I was born at Grassy Creek in Pendleton, Ky., twenty-fourth of February, 1833. My parents moved to Indiana when I was two years old. I came South in 1852 and at the time had a tolerably fair education. My uncle,

J. B. Thrasher, insisted on my taking a collegiate course, he paying all expenses. I started North with the intention of going to Princeton, N. J., but stopped in Indiana and graduated from the State University of that State at Bloomington in 1857. I then returned South and studied law in the office of my uncle, John B. During my college course at Bloomington I became engaged to be married to a young lady by the name of Margaret A. Borlsnd. I returned in 1859 and we were married in that year. I wanted to come South to live but she would not consent and we settled at Shelbyville, where I commenced the practice of law. She died in August 1860, having given birth to twin children a few days preceeding her death. I was then alone and my children died a few days after. Settling up my affairs, in September of that year I returned South to make my home at Port Gibson. I immediately commenced to practice and at the March term, 1861, of the Circuit Court had a pretty good docket, but the was breaking out shortly afterwards arrested everything. In July, I volunteered in the Claiburne Guards and served in the Twelfth Mississippi Regiment in Virginia, during the war. I fought in the ranks as a private; had no desire to assume the responsibilities of an officer. I was in all the principal battles fought in Virginia, Maryland and Pennsylvania; was wounded five times, but lived to resume the practice in connection with my uncle, J. B. Thrasher, in Port Gibson after hostilities had ceased. In the year 1875, I married Mrs. Lizzie Hamilton, widow of C. I. Hamilton. We have had no children, but she had some by her former husband and I think as much of them as if they were my own. I made a tolerable good fortune at the bar--quit the practice, went into other business and lost everything. Returned to the bar and made another comfortable sum of money. I quit the bar in 1886 and now live on my wife's plantation, about seven miles west of Port Gibson on the Mississippi River. I own a plantation of my own adjoining my wife's. I never had any taste for politics, but my friends ran me for the State Senate in 1885, and elected me without any difficulty. They conferred the honor on me again in 1889. I also served in the House, representing this and the adjoining county of Jefferson. My legislative life had existed for ten years. During the last session of the Legislature, I received nine votes in the caucus to fill the vacancy in the United States Senate caused by the resignation of General Walthall. These votes were altogether unsolicited and unexpected. I immediately arose, thanked my friends for the honor of their votes and positively declined to become a candidate. Had I done so, the probabilities are that I would have had as good a chance as the man who succeeded. This fact I learned after the selections had been made. I stood pretty fair at the bar and am known all over the State. I have a plantation of my own-- own a fifth interest in a "Cotton seed oil mill," representing a capital of two hundred thousand dollars. Stock in a bank and stock in other enterprises, besides other property, and etc. I am now a little past sixty-one years of age.

Stephen Thrasher.

Oak Lawn, Miss., March 31, 1894.

1808-1882.
AARON THRASHER----------------SUSAN ANDERSON.

THREE CHILDREN

O. P. THRASHER.   J. B. THRASHER.
            N. W. THRASHER.

(This sketch was furnished me by Mr. J. B. Thrasher, of
Demossville, Kentucky.)

AARON THRASHER was born in Pendleton County, Ky., in 1808, and died in 1882. His father was Stephen Thrasher (1762-1833), and his mother, Jane Powers, Stephen's second wife. In 1832, Aaron Thrasher married Miss Susanah N. Anderson, and lived with her till his death. Up to the year 1858 he was a farmer and miller then he went into merchandising at Demossville, Ky., which he followed till a short time before his death. He died in 1882, at the age of seventy-four, and his wife survived him two years. He was a man of sterling integrity, and held in high esteem in the community in which he lived. O. P. Thrasher, 1832, J. B. Thrasher, 1836, N. W. Thrasher, 1842.

1763-1849.   1769-1839.
JOSIAH THRASHER.................NANCY BONAR THRASHER.

SIX CHILDREN.

JOHN--1790-1879.   SALLY--1795.
WILLIAM--1792.   JAMES--1800.
AARON--1794.   STEPHEN--1804.

JOSIAH THRASHER (1763-1849), son of John and Elizabeth Hooker Thrasher, was born at Redstone, Md., January 23, 1763, and died in Fairview, Ind., August 8, 1849, in his eighty-seventh year. His wife, Nancy Bonar Thrasher, daughter of John and Criste Bonar, was born at Redstone, Md., March 30, 1769, and died at Fairview, Ind., February 1, 1839, aged seventy years. In 1789 they were married, and shortly after moved to Kentucky, where their six children were born. He, with his brothers, bought a large tract of land on Grassy Creek, and there located. His sons, John, William and Stephen moved to Rush County, Ind., in 1824, and a few years after (1830) he and his wife joined them. They lived with their son Stephen, south of Fairview, till 1839, when the wife died, and then Josiah went to live with his son John, west of Fairview. Here he died, and was buried beside his wife in the Fairview cemetery. He was of medium height, slightly bald, walked with crutches in consequence of chronic rheumatism, acquired in early life. He had a fiery temper, and when under the influence of liquor "feared neither man nor the devil." When once keeping a public house in Kentucky, he shot a bully who refused to pay for his drink. His wife was tall, slender, quiet, modest, ladylike person, just the opposite in temperament from her rollicking, roistering, and when under the influence of liquor, domineering

husband. The writer, when a boy often visited him. He was a jolly host, entertaining his guest with ripe apples, an egg cooked under the ashes in his old fire-place, a mug of cider, or droll anecdotes. We remember well the day he died. It was August 8, 1849. The writer a seven-year-old lad, with a brother and two cousins, were playing war in the orchard, with apples. They had chosen sides, apples flew thick and fast, and, peering from behind trees, we would often get hit on the head, at which our adversary would emit a yell of triumph. One of the lady relatives, Aunt Lucinda, came out in the orchard, and quieted our boisterous enthusiasm by saying "Grand-daddy Dick is dying," Mrs. Caroline Rush Dimmett, aged 81, still living, writes me: "Josiah Thrasher, in politics was a Democrat. When drinking, which he occasionally indulged in, he was abusive and overbearing, but at other times he was polite, kind, and pleasant to all."

JOHN THRASHER (1790-1879), the eldest of the twelve children born to Josiah and Nancy Thrasher, was the writer's grandfather, and was known by him intimately and well. John Thrasher, was born in Falmouth, Ky., February 11, 1790, in the second year of Washington's administration. He received a liberal education in private schools. In the neighborhood lived the Rush's, an intelligent, well-to-do family. Peter Rush (1766-1824), was a Virginian, the son of Thomas Rush (1700-1770), and cousin of the celebrated Benjamin Rush (1745-1813), of Philadelphia, one of the signers of the Declaration of Independence, and one of the most distinguished physicians and scholars of his time. John Thrasher married Elizabeth, the oldest daughter of Peter Rush (1766-1824), and Mary Mullins Rush (1777-1859). Mary Mullins Rush, the writer's great grandmother, traced her ancestry back to William Mullins (1575-1621), one of the "Mayflower" pilgrims and a man of wealth and influence. Elizabeth (1795-1855) was a round-faced handsome girl, with large beautiful eyes, and but sixteen years of age when led to the altar by her boyish sweetheart. They were married February 28, 1811. Ten children were born to them, as follows:

```
         1790-1878                      1795-1855
    JOHN THRASHER------------------------ELIZABETH THRASHER.
                        TEN CHILDREN.
```

WOODSON WALKER, Feb. 9, 1812.   JOSIAH, March 13, 1823.
MARY (known as Polly) Nov. 19, 1813. SARAH WALLER, Jan. 1, 1826.
NANCY, April 11, 1816.   LUCINDA, May 17, 1828.
WILLIAM P., August 25, 1818.   CAROLINE, March 22, 1832.
MARIA LOUISA, January 25, 1821.   JOSEPH, June 22, 1834.

Elizabeth was a woman of great decision of character, and governed her family with the austerity of a Roman matron. She possessed a high sense of fidelity and honor, and these principles she inculcated in her children. She was free spoken on questions of right and wrong, a devoted mother and Christian. She died in 1855, of what the village physician diagnosed as cancer of the stomach, in her sixtieth year, beloved by all. She was interred in the Fairview graveyard. In 1824 John Thrasher settled in Indiana. He and his family were the earliest of the Abolitionists of the country. On their coming they freed their slaves. One house slave James Van Horne,

emigrated with them. Van Horne settled on government land near Connersville, where he lived sixty years and more a respected and honored citizen. He raised quite a large family, many of them still live in that vicinity. John Thrasher was quiet and gentle, and possessed none of the turbulent and excitable traits of his father. Indeed, so mild and conservative was he that his wife and elder children chiefly took charge of affairs. In early life he was thrown from a horse, producing a hernia, which obliged him to wear a truss, and this possible prevented him from actively engaging in farm management. He was large hearted and hospitable, as Kentuckians are wont to be, and no one was turned away from his door hungry. He was reliable, honest and honorable, but preferred the retirement and quiet of his own home and surroundings, rather than be a participant in revolutionizing public affairs. He was not deficient, however, in public spirit, but preferred others to lead. After his wife's death he lived for a time with his eldest son--the writer's father--Woodson W. Thrasher. Growing tired of this kind of life, he married a widow, Mary Copeland, with whom he lived several years. When the helplessness of old age came, they peacefully separated, she to reside with a child by a former marriage, and he to live with his youngest son, Joseph Thrasher, in Cambridge City, Ind. He lived till death overtook him, in the year 1879, in the ninetieth year of his age. An odd idea seized him several years before he died. He bought his coffin, then the clothes he was to be buried in, and had them at hand to be used when needed. The clothing was a light summer suit, which led his waggish grandson, John, to say, "that grandfather evidently anticipates journeying to a warm climate."

```
              1812-1886              1811-1890
WOODSON W. THRASHER------------BARBARA THRASHER.
                      EIGHT CHILDREN
WILLIAM--1833.                        HARRIET--1844.
ELIZABETH--1836.                      SARAH--1847.
JOHN--1838.                           ALLEN--1851.
MARION--1842.                         OLIVE--1855.
```

WOODSON WALKER THRASHER (1812-1886), the writer's father, was a man of sturdy integrity, of probity, irreproachable in character, and most jealous of his honor. His word was infallible. He had the discipline and severity of a Puritan in his family government. He married in 1832 Barbara Daubenspeck, a well-to-do young Kentucky girl, he being in his twenty-first year and she nearly a year older. She had sufficient money to buy their home place at Fairview, Ind., in which they lived for thirty years and reared to manhood and womanhood a family of eight children. (Barbara Daubenspeck's mother was a Smelser, one of the most prominent families of Kentucky.) God never gave a tenderer hearted mother to children than she. She was one of the purest minded of women. She was utterly unselfish, charitable in the extreme, ever mindful of others' wants rather than her own. She sprang from a family noted for its longevity, an aunt living one hundred and four years, an uncle a century, while she has now (1895) a brother living, Jacob Daubenspeck (1796) nearly one hundred, and a sister, Lizzie Rush, (1804) who is in her ninetieth year. She died in 1890, honored and loved by the community in which she had lived sixty years and more. We cannot give a better idea of Woodson W. Thrasher's life and work than by quoting his biography, published in the "History of Fayette County, Ind."

"Honorable Woodson W. Thrasher, farmer, Fairview Township, was born in Pendleton County, Ky., February 4, 1812. His parents, John and Elizabeth (Rush) Thrasher, were natives of Kentucky, and of English and Irish extraction. John Thrasher was a son of Josiah Thrasher, a native of Maryland, and his father, John Thrasher, Sr., was one of three brothers who emigrated from England to the United States during the Revolutionary War. They settled in Maryland in 1750. He first settled in Maryland, and was there married to Elizabeth Hooker, and subsequently moved to Kentucky, where he remained until his death. He was a soldier in the Revolutionary War; was the father of a large family, of whom Josiah (the grandfather of our subject) was the eldest. (Stephen was the eldest.--Ed.) Josiah was married in Pendleton Co., Kentucky., to Nancy Bonar, and about the year 1830, moved to Rush Co., Ind., where she died shortly afterward. He survived her several years. Their children were John, Josiah, Sarah, and Stephen. (John, William, Aaron, Sarah, James, and Stephen.--Ed.) John Thrasher and Elizabeth daughter of Peter and Mary Rush, were united in wedlock in Pendleton, Ky., and in 1824 moved to Rush Co., Ind., where she died in 1855.

He subsequently married Mary Copeland, and died in 1879. He was the father of ten children: Woodson W., Mary, Nancy, William, Josiah, Maria, Lucinda, Caroline, Joseph, and an infant son who died unnamed. Our subject, with his parents, moved to Rush County, Ind., in 1824, and resided with them until his marriage, in 1831, with Barbara, daughter of Philip and Barbara Daubenspeck, born in Bourbon County, Ky., February 14, 1811. After his marriage, Mr. Thrasher settled just over the line from his father, in Fayette County, where he has since resided, giving his attention to agricultural pursuits, having been extensively engaged in breeding and raising improved stock; and to him are the people of this section of Indiana largely indebted for the fine stock with which the farms abound. He has as prominently, too, been connected with all enterprises and interests of the county which have had a tendency to develop the resources and to educate and Christianize her people. The subjects of education and Christianity have ever been close to his heart, and to their advancement he has given much of his mighty energy and liberally of his means, being largely instrumental in establishing the academy at Fairview and the Christian Church near by, with which both himself and wife have been connected for forty years or more, he having been an Elder therein during a greater part of the time. As an evidence of his interest in the subject of education, we have but to state that all his eight children are collegiate graduates, and among them are a prominent physician in Cincinnati, a professor of mathematics in Butler's College at Indianapolis, and another a graduate of the profession of law. The father of Mr. Thrasher before him was a Whig, with which party our subject was in his younger life identified, casting his first vote for Henry Clay. Since the organization of the Republican party he has been a warm advocate of its principles. He at one time was one of the County Commissioners, and in 1867 was chosen by the citizens of the county a Representative in the State Legislature, where he at once became conspicuous, and was identified with the leading measures that came before the Legislature during his term of service in the years 1867 and 1868. He was Chairman of the Committee on Roads and Highways; he also served on a committee appointed to visit and report the condition of the Southern prison at Jeffersonville; the Chairman's report he refused to sign, and, with another colleague, drew up a minority report, which was accepted by the Legislature. He was largely instrumental in securing the passage of the Indiana drain or ditching law, enacted during his service, which bill he was greatly interested in. His name is also connected prominently with other important measures, which, for want of space, we must leave unmentioned. Mr. Thrasher has been evidently successful in life, and had been blessed with most excellent health. Seldom, if ever, has he been confined to bed during his long life, on account of sickness; and it is greatly to his credit to remark that he has never been engaged in a lawsuit. He started in life with but small means, but by the thrift and industry he has accumulated a handsome competency. His children all grew to manhood and womanhood. Their names are William M., Elizabeth, John P., Marion, Harriet, Sarah, Allen B., and Olive."

1833.

WILLIAM MERRIT THRASHER--------DINIA THAYER.

FOUR CHILDREN.

CORINNE.   SALLIE.
WADE.   RAYMOND.

(Wm. M. Thrasher, A. M., an eminent professor of mathematics in Butler University, Indianapolis, for thirty years past, sends me an auto-biographical sketch, that I cannot resist publishing entire.)

AUTO-BIOGRAPHY OF W. M. THRASHER.

"I was born July 26, 1833, at Fairview, Fayette County, Ind. My earliest recollections pertain to the clearing up of a new farm. Log rollings, burning the heaps, gathering brush, building fence, feeding from 100 to 300 hogs, plowing corn, cutting wheat with sickle and cradle--these are my ancient history. We recovered fire with knife and flint, or went to the neighbors for a brand! I visited, at age of five, a log schoolhouse half a mile west of Fairview, of which only the memory remains of getting into a yellow-jacket's nest, and playing horse. My early teachers are chiefly remembered for their frequent application of the ferule and cat-o'nine-tails. Amusements of boyhood were bull pen, marbles, wrestling, jumping, invading melon patches and apple orchards, attending protracted meetings--chiefly outside the building, accompanying father on two or three annual squirrel hunts. My two first teachers, with whom I profited, were Robert Gordon and Merchant Kelly. Kelly bristled with a thousand corners--each giving out instruction. He made everything on earth, air and sky, as well as his innumerable inventions, the subject of instructive talks. At the age of fifteen, A. R. Benton, from Cato, N. Y., an 1848 graduate of Bethany, Brooks County, W. Va., and for one year a teacher in Woodward High School, Cincinnati, came to Fairview seeking employment as teacher. He had come on a visit to his old classmate, E. S. Frazee, who informed him that Fairview was a noted centre of Disciples of Christ. He opened a select school in one room on Doctor Clifford's premises with about twenty students. I, here, began the study of Latin and Greek. W. W. Thrasher, Greenbury Rush, John Shawhan employed Josiah Smith to build a brick academy building, into which, on its completion, was transferred Professor Bento n's school. His students soon embraced 50 to 100 from a half dozen States, and among them many men of promise and several of fulfillment. Debating clubs were organized. Robert Kidd, a promising elocutionist from California, convulsed select audiences with laughter at his inimitable comic impersonations, and other events of social and intellectual import followed. In September, 1853, my father, William Frazee, James Van Horn (colored) and myself, visited Bethany College: via Sandusky, Niagara, New York, Philadelphia, Baltimore, Washington City. I spent one year here and took the first honors of my class in four out of the five departments of the college.

(29)

To witness the graduating exercises, my father and D. R. Van Buskirk came to Bethany. At the close of the year, during a protracted meeting conducted by Alex Campbell and Isaac Errett, I entered the Christian Church. Returning home in July, 1854, I began a select school in a new academy at Fayetteville, Ind., at a better salary, teaching in the basement of the Christian Church. This was in 1858. In 1859, I visited Missouri and taught five months at Farmington, St. Francois County. Plenty of students but no money here caused my return to Fairview, where I taught three years, marrying in the meantime Miss Demia Thayer of Shelby County, Ind. In 1864 I taught at Rushville, whence in March, 1865, I was called to the professorship of mathematics in the Northwestern Christian University, Indianapolis, which position I now retain. In 1870 Indianapolis experienced a real estate boom, one of the results of the phenomenal prosperity which followed the Civil War. I made several thousand dollars, obtained leave of absence for two years, and August 30, 1873, embarked with my family and brother Allen, who had just graduated, for Heidelburg, Germany. We spent one delightful year in this beautiful town, disturbed only by the long illness of our youngest boy, Wade Thrasher. While here I visited the Rhine, took steamer from Mayence to Cologne enjoying much the historic castles and town along this famous stream. Returning, we visited Frankfort, Worms, Maunheim; visiting in the first the birth-house of Goethe, the Inden-gasse, the street of the Rothschilds: in the second, the Luther monument and the old cathedral famous for standing on the site of a former one, the scene of a duel described in the old German poem, the Nibelungen Lied. We made innumerable pedestrian tours in the neighborhood of Heidelburg, passing many days in and around the ruins of the old castle, probably the most interesting ruin, architecturally in Germany. We often sat, listening to lectures by Professor Kirchhoff of Chair of Physics, known for his invention of the spectroscope, and by Professor Bunsen, the chemist, famous the world over for his scientific discoveries. In October, 1873, I visited Vienna, Austria, via Stuttgart, Ulm, Augsburg and Saltzburg. Here we spent a week looking at the Welt-Ausstellung or World's Exposition. In March, 1874, I made the tour of South Germany, Switzerland and Italy returning via Munich and the Brenner Pass in the mountains of the Tyrol. Going, we passed into Italy at Turin, through the Mont Cenis Tunnel. I enjoyed thoroughly the Historic spots I had read of from childhood. I visited Genoa, with its Columbus monument; Bologna and its university; Florence and its twin art galleries in the Uffizi and Pitti palaces on opposite banks of the river Arno; Pisa and its leaning tower of white marble, and the cathedral in which swings today the lamp which suggested to Galilleo the pendulum; Rome with its St. Peters, its Coliseum, its Appian Way, its aqueducts and Pantheon; Naples with its adjacent Vesuvius and Baiae, the resort of the fashion of Rome; Venice and its square of St. Mark, its Bridge of Sighs, its canals, gondolas and Rialto; Verone and its amphitheatre and the garden of the scene between Romeo and Juliet; Milan with its cathedral, a symphony in marble. In March, 1875, we left Heidelburg for Paris via Strassburg. We ascended the cathedral at the latter place and from its roof, 250 ft. high, got an extended view of Rhine Valley.

We spent six weeks in Paris, threaded most of the streets, parks and gardens and cemeteries. We enjoyed the splendid art galleries of the Louvre, whose contents were mostly stolen from Italy by Napoleon. We then crossed the channel from Dieppe to New Haven and thence to London, where we spent a week visiting the parks, palaces, club houses, Westminster, the tower, the museum, the national Gallery. We visited also the old exposition building, the Crystal Palace at Sydenham. Then, via Rugby and Liverpool, we reached our steamer for New York, the "Egypt." I learned much, while abroad, of the resources for studying mathematics in English French and German. After returning, I spent several years in careful study of the classics in the higher mathematics in these three languages. We removed, in 1876, with the college, to Irvington, where we since reside. We have five children; three girls, Corinne, Nettie and Sally Blanche; two boys, Allen Wade and Raymond. Corinne became Mrs. Orville Carvin, residing at Irvington, and Sally the wife of A. J. Brown of Grand Rapids, Mich. Mr. Carvin travels for the firm of Fahnley, McCrea & Co., Indianapolis, while Mr. Brown is a wholesale and retail seedsman. In 1887 I planted a ten-acre ranch in Riverside navel oranges at Riverside in Southern California hoping to receive from it an income in old age." Wade is a physician in Indianapolis.

LIZZIE THRASHER (1836-1884), the next child, was educated at the Fairview Academy. She married at eighteen, Jas. P. Orr of Cincinnati, a schoolmate. He was a genius, and had enough talent for a half a dozen men. He was an eloquent minister; a Normal School Principal at Cincinnati, a surgeon in the Civil War; an orange-grower in Florida; Lizzie died at the writer's house in Cincinnati of typhoid fever in 1884, having just returned from Florida. She was distinguished for her charity and hospitality. She left a husband and but one child, a son, Ovid Orr, who is now a physician. A Cincinnati paper of that date thus speaks of her death: "Lizzie Thrasher Orr, the noted Sunday-school worker, died yesterday at Milford, beloved by all who knew her."

JOHN P. THRASHER (1838), was the second son of Woodson W. Thrasher, born in 1838, and was educated at the Fairview Seminary, under Prof. A. R. Benton. In 1862 he married Miss Lou Walker of Cincinnati, a young woman of lovely character, who has made for him an ideal home. They have been blessed with four children, two dying in infancy, and two surviving. Ada, born January 27, 1875, now an attractive young lady, and a graduate in the village Seminary; and George, born February 22, 1867, a successful young merchant in Oklahoma. I will give a brief extract of John's life as furnished me by himself:

"I graduated at the Cincinnati Law School in 1858. Practiced law in 1859-60 at Kokoma, Ind. Volunteered in the Sixteenth Regiment, Ind. Vol. Infantry, in April, 1861, and served one year; was a private for the first three months; then was promoted to "Brigade Ordinance Sargeant," and served in that capacity until mustered out at Washington, D. C., in May, 1862. Since that time I have lived on my farm at Fairview."

MARION THRASHER (1842), the writer, was born in Fayette Co., Ind., on March 13, 1842. He attended the village schools and seminary, subsequently the University (N. W. C.) at Indianapolis, Ind. In 1862-63, he attended the Medical Department of the University of Michigan, and in 1864-65, practiced medicine in Raleigh, Ind. In 1864, married Miss Sarah Murray, a daughter of James Murray, and grand-daughter of Prof. James Alexander Murray, an old Glasgow professor, and schoolmate of Carlyle's. Two children have been born to them--Clarence, who died in infancy in 1866, and Carroll, born in 1876. The following biographical sketch is taken from "Hoag's California":

"Dr. Marion Thrasher was born in Indiana, graduated at Butler University, and was for years a College Professor. He began his medical studies under his brother-in-law, Dr. James P. Orr of Cincinnati, took a medical degree in the University of Michigan, and subsequently graduated in the medical department of the University of California. He is a member of the San Francisco Medical Society, and the American Medical Association. He has frequently contributed medical theses before the latter Association, which papers have been published in "The Journal of the American Medical Association." He has a wife, Mrs. S. W. Thrasher, the editor of the Search Light, a literary paper of some note. They have a son, Carroll, born August 9, 1876, now a senior in Trinity College." They live in San Francisco.

HARRIET THRASHER (1844-1874), was educated at the Fairview Seminary, Indiana. She married Doctor Samuel Bell, of Philadelphia, Ind. She died at the birth of her second child, in 1874. Her first child survived, Charles Bell, who is now a promising young physician of Cincinnati.

SARAH THRASHER (1847), the third daughter, graduated at Lebanon College, Ohio; married a schoolmate, Mr. A. W. Vandeman, June 9, 1874; moved to Nebraska, where he became a prominent educator. They subsequently located in Denver, Colo., where they now reside. They have had three children, Gracie Thrasher, Herbert Allen, and Carl Louis. Gracie died Jan., 4, 1881; Bert and Carl, aged 16 and 12.

ALLEN BENTON THRASHER (1851), graduated at Butler University, Indiana, spent some years in Europe in Heidelberg, returned and graduated in medicine at the Ohio Medical College, Cincinnati. He is now a widely known medical practitioner in Cincinnati and stands high among his medical confreres. He married, in 1888, Miss Edith Williams of Cincinnati, and they have three children, Barbara, Ruth and Corinne. They have a handsome home at Mr. Auburn, a Cincinnati suburb. They are both highly educated, have traveled extensively in this and foreign lands, are well mated, and have the rare faculty of enjoying life at its best.

OLLIE THRASHER (1855), received a seminary education, as the other children. She married Mr. Marshall Blacklidge, of Rushville, Ind., a young man from one of the best families of that section. They have a lovely home, and one child, a boy, Allen, born in 1891.

(32)

MARY THRASHER, eldest daughter of John and Elizabeth Thrasher was born in Kentucky, November 19, 1813. Moved to Indiana in 1824 with her parents. She married Jacob B. Power in October 17, 1833. They had five children, three girls and two boys; a girl and boy died young. Julius Power, a promising boy, born in 1843, entered the Rebellion and died of fever. Ester married Mr. Ball and has two children. Maria married Mr. Nickerson and has two children, girls.

1816-1886.	1816.
NANCY THRASHER (PRINE).	DANIEL S. PRINE.

EIGHT CHILDREN.

WILLIAM H.	JOHN W.
MARY J.	ELIZABETH P.
MATTHEW M.	NANCY C.
HARRIET A.	SARAH P.

(The following sketch sent by Mr. William H. Prine of Iowa.)

NANCY THRASHER (1816-1886), second daughter of John and Elizabeth Thrasher, was born in Pendleton County Ky., in 1816. At the age of eight she came to Rush County, Ind., with her parents. Here she was educated and on October 5, 1837, in her twenty-first year, she married Daniel S. Prine, a neighboring farmer's boy of good family. In 1850 they moved to Oskaloosa, Iowa, where she resided till her death, April 18, 1886, loved and respected by all who knew her. William Huston Prine was born February 16, 1839. Was married to Priscilla I Coffin, September 11, 1862. They have two children, Lillie I. and Eva R. Lillie was born in 1864 and married in 1888 to John M. Jackson and now reside at Colorado Springs. They have two children, Ray and Grace, aged eight and four. Eva R. was born in 1872. Mary J. Prine was born in 1840; married George W. Corwin in 1862. Have two children, Russel and Rella, both married. Russel married Miss Williams in 1890, and has one son, Russel. Rella married Mr. Roberts. Matthew M. Prine was born in 1843 and married Emma J. Turner in 1879. They have one son, Homer, born in 1879. Harriet A. Prine, born in 1845, married Charles H. Rodgers in 1869. They had two children, Estella, born in 1871, died in 1873, and Frank, born in 1876. Harriet A. Prine died in 1879. John W. Prine (1851). Elizabeth P. Prine, born in 1849, married Jacob M. Hines in 1870. They have one son, George, born in 1877. Nancy C. Prine, born in 1852, married Samuel L. Lathrop in 1885. Have one son, Ray, born in 1890. Mr. Lathrop shot and killed himself accidentally when Ray was two weeks old. Sarah P. Prine, born in 1858, married Jacob M. Turner, 1884. Have no children.

(Mr. W. L. Thrasher sends me the following biography of his father and family:)

WILLIAM P. THRASHER (1818-1862), son of John and Elizabeth Thrasher, was born in Kentucky, August 25, 1818; killed in the late war August 30, 1862, at Richmond, Ky., the father of ten children,

seven boys and three girls, whom four are living at this date, November 15, 1893. Woodson W. Thrasher, son of William P. Thrasher and Elizabeth Parrish Thrasher, was born December 11, 1840, and the father of three children, two living and one dead. The youngest, a son, William Levi Thrasher, was born May 17, 1866, the father of one son. Henry R. Thrasher, son of William and Elizabeth Thrasher, was born November 3, 1847, the father of six children, two boys and four girls. Amos M. Thrasher, son of Wm. and Elizabeth Thrasher, was born May 27, 1845. Caleb Thrasher, son of Wm. and Elizabeth Thrasher, born January 20, 1850, died September 3, 1857. John M. Thrasher, son of same above, born June 28, 1852, died, November 12, 1859. James W. Thrasher, son of same, born August 24, 1855, died, December 15, 1859. Caylor Thrasher, son of William and Elizabeth Thrasher, born March 10, 1857, died Nov., 15, 1859. Amanda Nelson, daughter of William and Elizabeth Thrasher, born June 5, 1838, died, July 4, 1882. Adeline W. Caylor, daughter of William and Elizabeth Thrasher, born January 18, 1843, died November 8, 1865. Mother of three children, one son and two daughters. Mary Ooty Bagwell, daughter of William and Elizabeth Thrasher, born April 2, 1859. Mother of eight children, four living and four dead.

William P. Thrasher, carpenter; Woodson W. Thrasher, merchant; Henry K. Thrasher, farmer; Amos M. Thrasher, railroad man; William L. Thrasher, breeder of poultry.

Maria Thrasher was born in 1821. Married Robert T. Wells in 1845, and died in Fairview, Ind., of cancer, in 1855, leaving five children.

Josiah Thrasher was born March 13, 1823. Married Amanda McConnell, September 5, 1844. They moved to Rigdon, Ind. They had several children, but only five reached maturity. Nancy married Mr. Noble, Mary married Mr. Behymer, and Leonidas, Martha and Minnie.

Sarah Waller Thrasher, daughter of John and Elizabeth Thrasher was born June 1, 1826. She was married to Robert Gordon, a school teacher of some note, October 15, 1848. They had but one child that reached adult age, and that was George, who became a physician. Dr. George Gordon married, practiced Medicine at Centerville, Ind., and had one child, a boy.

Lucinda Thrasher, daughter of John and Elizabeth Thrasher, was born May 17, 1828, married Mr. Harvey M. Piner, a young man from one of the wealthiest families in the neighborhood, on January 22, 1852. They have two children, Quincy and Edward, both married. Quincy has two children. Edward's wife died recently without issue.

Caroline Thrasher, daughter of John and Elizabeth Thrasher, was born March 22, 1832, married Mr. William A. Patterson, April 6, 1851. Have three children, viz.: John, ------, ------.

Joseph Thrasher, son of John and Elizabeth Thrasher, was born June 22, 1834, college educated, and became a teacher of marked ability, married Miss Emma Williams, Sept., 7, 1856, and had three children--Ida, married to Mr. Ronzhoff, and lives at Indianapolis, Watkins and Emma. Entire family dead except Ida.

William, Aaron, Sally, and James, we have been unable to satisfactorily trace.

Stephen Thrasher went to Indiana, and settled south of Fairview, married Miss Mary McCarthy, and reared to maturity three children, Lizzie (1834), John (1838), and Charles (1842). In 1845 Stephen lost his life by a foot injury. His wife died in 1885. John and Lizzie live on the home-place, both unmarried, while Charles is married and lives in Wheeling, W. Va.

(Too late for Classification.)

EPISTOLARY CORRESPONDENCE WITH DIVERGING BRANCHES OF
THE THRASHER FAMILY.

(Wm. F. Thrasher was the son of John Thrasher (1801-188-) and
grandson of the John Thrasher (1730-1806), probably, who came
from Wales in 1750 to Redstone, Maryland, and in 1792 to Kentucky near Lexington. The father of Wm. F. Thrasher had three
brothers, Elias, Stephen and Eli, and four sisters. All are
dead except Eli, who resides at Lewiston, Mo., aged eighty-four.)

Burlington, Iowa, December 11, 1894.

Marion Thrasher, M. D.,
San Francisco, Cal.

Dear Sir: I was born in Marion County, Mo., the sixth of June,
1840; my wife, Sarah E. Gregory was born in Lewis County, Mo.,
September 24, 1840. I was married November 8, 1860. John D.,
our son, was born September 13, 1861. Susie Cally was born July
21, 1867, but died January 4, 1893. Alpha was born March 10,
1874. We had eight children in all, the rest dying in infancy.
I am District Agent of the Union Building and Savings Association,
located at Des Moines, Iowa.

I have a sister Sarah, Samuel Miller's wife, of Palmyra,
Marion County, Mo. Have an uncle, Eli Thrasher, of Lewiston,
Lewis County, Mo. My other sister, Jala McRea, lives at Gage,
Texas. I have the honor of remaining,

Yours truly,
W. F. Thrasher.

Springwood, Va., November 5, 1894.

Doctor Marion Thrasher,

My Dear Sir: I am a "Thrasher" born and raided in Virginia.
Name, John Q. A. Thrasher; will be seventy years old January 25,
1895. My grandfather came from Germany, he and one brother, and
settled in Pennsylvania. My father was born there, moved to
Maryland when two years old, lived there sixteen years, moved to
Botetourt County, Va., where he spent the remainder of his days.
Grandfather's family are all dead. My oldest sister is eighty-
five years old, Mrs. Margaret Lines, lives with her son, Dr. F.
Lines, Fort Wayne, Ind. My second sister, Mrs. Adeline Zimmer-
man, eighty-three years old, living in Fincastle, Botetourt County,
Va. My third sister, seventy-four years old, Mrs Mary McCartney,
living in Craig County (address Ripley Mills). My fourth sister,
sixty-eight years old, Mrs. Susan Firebaugh, living near Fincastle,
Botetourt County, Va. My father's family consisted of twelve children. I am the eighth child. I have a nephew merchandizing in
Springwood, Botetourt County, Va., named W. T. Thrasher. Also, I

have a nephew living near Lithia, Botetourt County, Va., name
J. M. Thrasher. With regards, I am,

        J. Q. A. Thrasher,
      Springwood, Botetourt County, Va.

(The following furnished me by Mrs. Johnie Travis Thrasher
O'neal, of Dothan, Ala., traces J. Cloud Thrasher's family--
J. Cloud Thrasher being a son of David Thrasher (1796-1882).)

       Dothan, Ala., November 16, 1894.

Dear Cousin:
  As Papa (John Thomas Thrasher) was too busy to write, he
asked me to give you as much information as we could. The family record is at Jacksonville, Fla. Papa's stepmother has it,
Mrs. C. V. Thrasher, care of E. J. Blaire. James Cloud Thrasher
was first married to Nancy Travis. (See record at Jacksonville.)
They had six children. John Thomas Thrasher was born in Newton
County, Ga., in 1874, February 15. In 1868 he was married to
Ophelia Reynolds, daughter of Captain A. M. Reynolds, at Jefferson, Jackson County, Ga. They have six children, three girls
and three boys. Jessie May Thrasher was born at Lake City, Fla.,
September 5, 1869. She was married to Wallace M. Hunter, of
Catskill, N. Y., in April 24, 1889, at Quitman, Ga. They have
two children--Ophelia Hunter was born at Quitman, Ga., in 1890,
March 20. Mary Essie Hunter was born at Quitman, Ga., November
12, 1892. They live now in Dothan. James Munroe Thrasher was
born in Thomas County, Ga., January 19, 1871. He was married to
Maggie L Barnes, of Quitman, Ga., on April 26, 1890. Maggie
Thrasher died July 12, 1892, at Quitman. Annie lives with her
grandfather, John Thrasher. Mary Thrasher was born at Quitman,
Ga., July 24, 1873; was married to Dr. W. I. Johnson, of Troy,
Ala., October 11, 1893. They live in Dothan. Johnie Travis
Thrasher was born September 10, 1875, at Quitman, Ga. She was
married July 8, 1894, to W. C. O'Neal, of Dothan, Ala. David
Barton Thrasher was born at Quitman, Ga., March 11, 1879. Jelks
Reynolds Thrasher was born at Quitman, October 17, 1881. I'll
give you all I can of the other children of grandfather. Mary E.
Thrasher, in 1848, and died at Lake City, Fla., 1865 or 1866.
Nancy Rebecca Thrasher was born about 1850. Was married to C. W.
Henry about 1870; died 1882, leaving one girl and four boys. For
their births and ages write to Joe Henry, Jacksonville, Fla.;
E. J. Blaire. David Barton Thrasher was born 1852. I think was
married to Annie Rountree at Quitman in 1871. They have five boys
the little girl died about two months ago. For their address E.
B. Thrasher, Jacksonville, Fla. Jesse Whitfield Thrasher was born
in 1854; was married to Jennie McMullen, in 1877, and has two
girls and five boys. Write to J. W. Thrasher, Quitman, Ga. James
Buckhanan Thrasher was born about 1856, was burned to death, 1859,
by following cook to wash pot. Grandfather's second wife was

Catherine F. Hughey. She has four children by their union; the two boys are dead; the two girls are married, and have three or four children each--Mrs James Canter and Mrs. T. J. Blaire, Jacksonville. Grandfather, J. Cloud Thrasher, died September 23, 1879, in Newton County, Ga., and was buried at the Thrasher Cemetery, Sincerely,

Mrs. W. C. O'Neal.

1796-1843.
JOSEPH THRASHER

Fountaintown, Ind.,
October 17, 1894.

Dr. Marion Thrasher,

Dear Cousin: In reply to yours of the 29th ult.--Joseph's children: Meredith, born April 14, 1819, married Elizabeth Walker. His children were John, Mary and Elizabeth. I do not know the date of his death nor the whereabouts of his children. Mary, born July 6, 1821, married to William Brown, a merchant of Shelbyville; had only one child, died in infancy. Elizabeth, born Feb., 21, 1823, married to Luke Davis February 1, 1844; two children, Allen and Eva--I presume you are acquainted with both of them; Eva is at Aunt Caroline's, near Falmouth, and Allen is at Shelbyville. Alfred, born June 13, 1825; died November 22, 1825. Leonidas L. born August 18, 1827; married Frances Perry May 4, 1848; was a civil engineer by trade; four children, Melissa, Milton, Alice and Milburn. Leonidas served through the Mexican War, and at the breaking of the Civil War raised a company and went out as First Lieutenant, Third Ind. Battery, Light Artillery; served with distinction; promoted to captaincy. At present he is stationed at the Soldier's Home, Marion, Ind., having been transferred from Dayton, O. Melissa was married to George Campbell, a farmer near Shelbyville. Her two children are Walter and Allie. Milton is married, but to whom. I do not know; he belongs to the firm of S. B. Morris & Co.; his address is Shelbyville, Ind.; write to him, he can inform you on the history of his father and sisters and brothers better than I. Alice married a farmer by the name of Weir, Frank Weir, a well-to-do farmer; live near Acton, Ind. Milburn is unknown; supposed to be in Texas. Napoleon B., born October 12, 1830, died April 12, 1877; unmarried; a weaver by occupation; served through the Civil War as bugler; was out five years and three months.

William R., born in Shelbyville, Ind., February 21, 1832; carpenter by trade; married Naomi J. Kennedy; four children, Joel, Tressie, Robert and Naomi: only one survives, Tressie; by William R's second marriage to Emily C. Moore, March 23, 1862, nine children, Versylia O., born February 3, 1863, married to T. H. Tadlock, a blacksmith, at Noah, December 25, 1885; have four children, Ernest, Fannie, Willie, and Mary. W. W., born December 26, 1864, married Sale A. Scotton, at Indianapolis, July 31, 1893; carpenter.

Fannie B., born November 30, 1866; married to S. F. T. Steirs August 18, 1866; blacksmith at Little Blue. Samuel L., born June 6, 1869; married Ida Nichols, June 15, 1890. John B., born April 13, 1871; blacksmith by trade. Charles M., born August 1, 1874. Jesse A., born February 12, 1877. Albert d., born July 18, 1879. Stella M., bo rn July 31, 1882. John, bo rn August 11, 1834, married Sarah A. La Favers; two children, Maggie and Matilda; served in the late war; died at Nashville, Tenn., during service. Joseph, born January 4, 1837; married to Melvina La Favers; two children, Melvyna and Melvin; Melvin is a painter by trade. Malinda M., born January 31, 1840; married to John Perry, a carpenter; two children, Forrest and Fannie. I am glad to know who your father was. I know how closely we are related. The above are my grandfather's children and their posterity. Below I will give you the names and addresses of all the Thrashers, or relatives to the Thrashers, excepting my own immediate family: Meredith's children I know nothing of; Allen Davis, Shelbyville, Ind.; Eva Irwin, Falmouth, Ind.; Melissa Campbell, Shelbyville, Ind.; Milton Thrasher, Shelbyville, Ind.; Alice Weir, Acton, Ind.; Maggie Williams, Shelbyville, Ind.; Matilda Thrasher, Shelbyville, Ind.; Melvin Thrasher, Shelbyville, Ind.; Fannie Jackson, Noah, Ind.; John Thrasher, Shelbyville, Ind.; William Little, Shelbyville, Ind: John and Nelson Thrasher, Richard and Benjamin Mullen, Demossville, Ky.; Richard Anderson, Butler, Ky.; William and Charles Thrasher, Indianapolis, Ins. There is a Reuben Thrasher in Colley, Pa., a dealer in musical instruments; I have been unable to trace him; perhaps it would be well to write him. We have relatives in New York City, and by writing to William Little, at Shelbyville, you can get their postoffice address. Any further information will be cheerfully given. My postoffice is Fountaintown, Ind. Info rmation to Noah, Ind., will reach me. I am truly,

W. W. Thrasher.

(The following received from Mary V. Thrasher Cherry of Canton, Mo., giving a brief history of the Thrasher family in Missouri.)

Canton, Mo., November 22, 1894.

Doctor Marion Thrasher,
Dear Cousin: My grandfather was John Thrasher; do not know the date of his birth or death; he had four daughters, all of whom are dead. Also, four sons--John, Elias, Stephen and Eli, all dead but Eli. John Thrasher lived in Marion County, this State; raised a large family of children--seven daughters and four sons. Uncle John has been dead several years, and only two daughters and two sons living. John Thrasher of Brashear, Adair Co., this State; William F. Thrasher of Burlington, Iowa. If you write to them you can get dates, and further particulars. Uncle Elias died many years ago, but I know left three sons by his first wife, namely; Elisha, Willis and John. They went to California in an early day. For awhile they wrote us, but have not heard from any

of them for a long time. Have been told Cousin Willis was the only one living, do not know his address. My father, Stephen F. Thrasher, was born in Kentucky in 1805; moved to Missouri in an early day, and located in Lewis County. He was twice married. First to Miss Lucinda Mullen, by whom he had three children, Issac, James and Sarah. His second wife (my mother), was Miss Sarah Rush, by whom he had six children--Mary V. (my name), Gabriel A., John W. Nancy F., Elizabeth M., Laura J.--in all five daughters and four sons. Father died in 1879. There are only two sons and three daughters living. Brother Isaac was a pilot on the Mississippi River, and died several years ago at Hannibal of small-pox. Brother J. M. Thrasher is living in Sullivan County, Mo.; his postoffice address is Winnegan; he has a large family of children, Sister Sarah Morris is living near Shelbina, Mo. She has two daughters. I had two children by my first husband--a son and daughter--both married. Brother G. A. Thrasher has been living in Kansas for several years, but is now living here; he has a family of five grown children, all sons but one. His address is Canton. Brother John W. also moved to Kansas years ago. In April 1889, went west, and since the following August we have not heard from him; we fear he is dead; he had two sons--one living in Oklahoma, and one in Arlington, Kansas. Sister N. F. Moffett is living in Kahoka, Clark County. She has a family of seven children--four daughters and three sons (interesting children). Sisters Elizabeth and Laura died in young womanhood. Uncle Eli is living, is about eighty-four and very poorly now. If you will address him at Lewiston, this County and State, you can get older records than I can give you. Your cousin,

M. V. Cherry.

1765.
ELIAS THRASHER.

(Elias Thrasher, one of the five brothers, went to Missouri, and had five sons, viz: John F., Elisha, Stephen, Willis, Eli. Joel F. Thrasher, of Hannibal, Mo., a grandson of John F., writes me of that branch of the family.)

November 4, 1694.

Mr. Marion Thrasher, M. D.,
    Dear Sir: The John F. Thrasher you spoke of was my grandfather. There were five brothers--John F., Elisha, Stephen, Willis, Eli; all of these are dead but Eli. His Post Office is Lewiston, Lewis County, Mo. These all came from near Lexington, Ky. John F., had four sons, Tommy, John R., Joel, William, of whom Tommy and Joel are dead. John R., postoffice, Brashear, Adair County, Mo. William, postoffice, Burlington, Iowa. Elisha I cannot give you any information about. Stephen had two sons. I think you can get all the information about them by writing to Mary Cherry, at Canton, Mo. Of Willis, I cannot give any information. Eli had six sons, John, George, William, Ira, Sam, Frank, all living. John, George, Ira, and Frank are living

near Lewiston, Lewis County, Mo. Cannot give you William or Sam's address. Sons of John F., four. Tommy, I cannot give the number of his sons, but write to John Thrasher, Brashears, Adair Co., Mo., for information. John R., one son; he is in California. Joel had three sons, John F., Porter, Joel F.; Porter is dead; John F., postoffice, Broway, Hannibal, Mo.; Joel F., Hannibal, Mo. William, of Burlington, Ia., had two sons living near his father's. There are still smaller children, but none of age.

       I am respectfully yours,
       Joel F. Thrasher, Hannibal, Mo.

(Dr. J. Dorsey Thrasher of Forest Hill, W. Va., sends me the following, relative to his branch of the family in Virginia.)

      Forest Hill, W. Va., November 22, 1894.

My great great grandfather Thrasher was born in Germany and came to Bereloay County, Virginia, now West Virginia. I cannot find out his name. His sons were Powell, Mike, Conrad, George and Fredric. All of them settled in Virginia. Fredric, my great grandfather, was born in Virginia, September 21, 1769; married Nancy Filson in April, 1794, and died 1852. He was a farmer and father of the following children: Margaret, born April 2, 1796; Stafle, born February 2, 1798; Polly, born March 2, 1800; John, born October 22, 1802; Robert, born November 2, 1804; Sarah, born February 27, 1807; Anna, born July 26, 1809; Delila, born March 25, 1911; Rhodah, born July 10, 1813; Paul, born September 11, 1815. Robert Thrasher, my grandfather, born November 2, 1804, in Virginia, married Susan Campbell at Big Lich, Va., now Roanoke City, November 12, 1828; came to West Virginia two years later; settled in the forests of Monroe County: cleared a thousand-acre farm, which is now very valuable; died about May 1865; was father of the following children: Leroy C. Thrasher, born December 29, 1830; F. G. Thrasher, born November 24, 1834; C. R. Thrasher; Margaret M. Thrasher, born February 1836; Ann E. Thrasher, A. P. Thrasher, T. R. Thrasher. Leroy C. Thrasher, my father, born December 29, 1830, in Monroe County, W. Va.; graduated in medicine at Richmond Medical School, March, 1852; located at Red Sulphur Spring, W. Va., 1854, where he followed his profession with distinction until his death, January 29, 1880; married Lucy J. Thrasher, February 14, 1854; was father of the following children: J. Dorsey Thrasher, born May 14, 1860; R. E. Thrasher, born June 18, 1864; O. L. Thrasher, born September 17, 1868. J. Dorsey Thrasher, born at Red Sulphur Springs, Monroe County, W. Va., May 14, 1860. Graduated in medicine at Richmond Medical School in 1876; located at Forest Hill, Summers County, W. Va., in June of same year; married Emma Campbell, January 2, 1881; is father of the following children: Horace C. Thrasher, born October 6, 1881; Claude L. Thrasher, born March 26, 1886; Dorsey Glenn Thrasher, born March 11, 1889, died September 16, 1891; Paul G. Thrasher, born December 31, 1892. Yours,

       J. Dorsey Thrasher, M. D.

(41)

Florence, Ala., Oct 13, 1894.

Doctor Marion Thrasher:

My grandfather, Elias Thrasher, came from England; he had two brothers, Thomas and George; Thomas went to Georgia, George to Alabama, and Grandfather Elias to Loudoun County, Va. My grandfather, Elias Thrasher, died in 1823, in Loudoun County, Va; do not know the date of his birth; he had the following children: Thomas, Luther, Malinda, Sarah Ann, Elias, Hanson, Archer, John, William B. L., and Amanda. My father's name was William B. L. Thrasher; his children were Pugh H., John C., Hattie Ann, Elias, Thomas, Emily, Elissie, Henson, Mike, James. I was married when thirty-five years old, to Miss Farmer; had six children, four only living: P. F. Thrasher in Texas, William B. in Arkansas; a daughter married a Thrasher, and lives here, and another married J. M. Williams. I was in the Federal army as Captain; am a mechanic; have been a widower seven years. Elias lived in Dayton, Ohio; Hanson in Florence, Alabama; Archer in Iola, Kansas; John in Maryland, and Wm. B. L., in Alabama.

      Truly yours, Elias Thrasher.

      Demossville, Ky., March 31, 1894.

Doctor Marion Thrasher:

Dear Sir: My father, Aaron Thrasher, was born in 1808, and died in 1882; he was married in 1832, to Miss Susannah N. Anderson, and lived with her until his death; she lived till 1884. His occupation was farming and milling until 1858, when he went into merchandizing and remained in the business until a short time before his death. He had four children; three boys lived to maturity; I will give their ages: O. F. Thrasher, 60 years; J. B. Thrasher, 58 years; E. W. Thrasher, 52 years. My grandfather's name was Stephen Thrasher, and he lived and died in Kentucky; he died in 1833; he had five brothers; they were all born at Redstone, Md., and then three came to Kentucky, one went to Georgia, and one to Arkansas. I will give you a list of my oldest aunts: Sarah Thrasher married Lahnahan Dougherty; Mary Thrasher married a man by the name of James Titus. My half-aunt's name was Elizabeth Thrasher; she married a man by the name of Richard Pugit From the best information that I can get they all came to Kentucky in 1793.

      Yours most respectfully,
      J. B. Thrasher.

(Sketch of Rev. G. B. Thrasher's life.)

My father Barton C. Thrasher died in 1876--my grandfather, Isaac Thrasher, died in 1878. Mattie Bishop, Watkinsville, Ga.; Ola Jackson, Winder, Ga.; Fannie Baxter, La Grange, Ga., are sisters of mine. My father's three brothers--Thomas, William, and John--are all dead.

Their families live in Oconee Co., Ga. The family have always been prolific and wherever they settled have stocked the earth. Yours,

G. B. Thrasher.

(From Mr. J. S. Thrasher, son of John James Thrasher (1818), "Cousin John," grandson of David Thrasher (1796-1882), great grandson of John Thrasher (1761-1840).)

Brunswick, Ga., October 29, 1894.

Dr. Marion Thrasher,
San Francisco, Cal.

Your card just received, which I shall answer as fully as I am able. First my father, known as "Cousin John" Thrasher, the founder of Atlanta, Ga., seventy-five years of age, is living at Pasadena, Fla. My grandfather, David Thrasher, died at the age of eighty-six, ten years since. His brothers, Barton and Isaac, are dead--died in this State. They all left many heirs. My father had eight children, Jesse S., Barton C., David O., Willis E., Johnnie J. (died at nine), Margaret V., Mary D., Ellen B. (dead). All the family reside in Florida but myself. My family live in Chattanooga, where I am rearing up a family of six--four girls and two boys: Paul, Siles, Mary B., Emma, Maggie D., and Ruth. We are Baptists; some of the name are Methodists. Father's family--four boys. I am fifty years old the twenty-seventh day of January, 1895. And I am glad to say that we were brought up in Atlanta, and were raised to manhood and womanhood, and no stain upon the character of the girls, and the boys so behaved as to avoid arrest or even suspicion of crime. Our father prior to the war was very rich for this country, and enjoyed, and still enjoys, a reputation that is very good indeed. Atlanta will tell you of his standing.

Respectfully, J. S. Thrasher.

Watkinsville, Ga., December 12, 1894.

Dr. Marion Thrasher,
San Francisco, Cal.,

My mother was Asyneth Thrasher, daughter of Barton Thrasher. She had six children--Ann Olivia, Mary Frances, Nicholas, Barton, Basil Earl, and Asyneth Caroline.

Very truly, B. E. Overby,
Sheriff of Oconee Co., Ga.

(Mr. James M. Thrasher, of Winigan, Mo., son of Stephen F. Thrasher (1805-1879), grandson of John Thrasher, sister of Mrs. Mary V. Thrasher-Cherry, of Canton, Mo., forwards me the following:)

Winigan, Mo., December 19, 1894.

Dr. Marion Thrasher,
San Francisco, Cal.

Dear Sir: I herewith give you the information requested. I was born September 17, 1832. I married Martha M. Pickerel February 15, 1855. She was born in Mason County, Ky., April 21, 1836. The names of my children are as follows: Isaac H., born December 31, 1855; Laura J., born March 21, 1856; Oliver C., born November 4, 1860; Joseph A., born November 24, 1862; Stephen H., born October 31, 1864; Martha F., born May 11, 1867; Minnie V., born January 23, 1869; Lillie B., born June 22, 1872; John W., born April 18, 1874. Laura J. married F. Greenstreet, Winigan, Mo.; Lillie B. Married J. H. Myers, Winigan Mo.; Minnie V. married A. Haselton, Loeffler, Mo.; Martha F. married W. A. Johnson, Viola, Mo. The P. O. address of all the boys is Winigan, Mo.
Respectfully,
James M. Thrasher.

(Mrs Thrasher-McRae, of Gage, Texas, a daughter of John Thrasher, of Marion County, Mo., and sister of Wm. F. Thrasher, of Burlington, Iowa, writes me of her own immediate family:)

I was married to S. C. McRae November 27, 1845; born November 17, 1828. I have nine children: Plinoh E., born September 6, 1848; Eliza F., born July 22, 1851; John T., born April 30, 1854; Mary V., born July 13, 1857; George W., born April 11, 1860; W. H., born February 19, 1863; Sarah N., born October 17, 1866; James P., born October 18, 1869; Charles M., born August 22, 1873. Mary V. McRae was married to J. K. Bruce September 25, 1881, Geo. W. McRae was married to Alice House January 30, 1891. J. P. McRae was married to Mary Armstrong December 23, 1891. W. H. McRae was married to Sallie L. Cherry April 9, 1885. Eliza McRae was married to Wm. Burnsford April 24, 1883.

(44)

Abbott, Mrs. Lucy, Atlanta, Ga.
Adair, Mrs. Bettie, Atlanta, Ga.
Alberson, Mr., Alpharatta, Ga.
Anderson, Richard, Butler, Ky.
Anderson, Mrs. Margaret, Atlanta, Ga.
Baxter, Fannie, La Grange, Ga.
Bell, Dr. Chas., Cincinnate, O.
Bishop, Mattie, Watkinsville, Ga.
Behymer, Mary Thrasher, Elwood, Ind.
Blanford, Mrs. David, Lewisport, Ky.
Blacklidge, Olive Thrasher, Rushville, Ind.
Bonzhof, Ida Thrasher, Indianapolis, Ind.
Camp, Mrs. D. C., Atlanta, Ga.
Campberr, Mrs. Melissa, Shelbyville, Ind.
Campbell, Tom, Lewisport, Ind.
Campberr, Mrs. Harriet, Cannelton, Ind.
Cherry, Mary V., Canton, Mo.
Crow, Mrs. Mat, Cora, Ga.
Davis, Allen P., Shelbyville, Ind.
Dimmett, Mrs. Caroline, Falmouth, Ind.
Erwin, Mrs. Elvera D., Falmouth, Ind.
Fegg, Tom, Grandview, Ind.
Gabbert, Eli, Grandview, Ind.
Golding, W. E., Shelbyville, Ind.
Gordon, Sarah Thrasher, Falmouth, Ind.
Gregory, Jno. S., Lewisport, Ky.
Gregory, Jas. Henry, Grissom's Landing, Daviess Co., Ky.
Gabbert, Columbus, Grandview, Ind.
Greer, Leonard, Choccolocco, Ala.
Gabbert, Woodson, Rockport, Ind.
Gunter, Mrs. Bettie, White House, Ga.
Harper, Mrs. Fannie, Camp Hill, Ala.
Harper, Mrs. Captain James, Camp Hill, Ala.
Higdon, R. G. Mrs., Calhoun, Ky.
Huffman, Mrs. Martha, Lewisport, Ky.
Hughey, David, Wilder, Ga.
Hughey, John, Jacksonville, Fla.
Hull Green, Conyers P. O., Ga.
Jackson, Barton, Wilder, Ga.
Jackson, Fannie, Noah, Ind.
Jackson, Fulton, Wilder, Ga.
Jackson, David, Grandview, Ind.
Jackson, Rev. Luther, Auburn, Ga.
Kelly, Martha, Lewisport, Ky.
Lear, Amanda Thrasher, Rigdon, Ind.
Little, William, Shelbyville, Ind.
Livingstone, Mrs. Clem., Cora, Ga.
Morgan, Ben E. Howard, Kas.
Miller, Abbie Thrasher, Hawesville, Ky.
Michel, Jennie, Cannelton, Ind.
Mullin, Richard, Demossville, Ky.
Mullin, Benjamin, Demossville, Ky.
Middlebrook, Barton, Farmington, Ga.

(45)

Noble, Nancy Thrasher, Orestes, Ind.
O'Neal, Johnnie Thrasher, Dothan, Ala.
Orr, Dr. Ovid, Cincinnati, Ohio.
Overby, Mrs Basil, Atlanta, Ga.
Overby, Mrs. Josephine, Farmington, Ga.
Pate, John Robert, Lewisport, Ky.
Pate, Samuel, Lewisport, Ky.
Pierce, Mrs. Jack, Conyers, Ga.
Piper, Lucinda Thrasher, Falmouth, Ind.
Powers, Jacob, Indianapolis, Ind.
Prine, William Huston, Oskaloosa, Iowa.
Reed, Mrs. Areyetta, Louisville, Ky.
Roe, Aretta, Hawesville, Ky.
Sample, Mrs. Hester, Lewisport, Ky.
Sawyer, Mrs. Dave, Armiston, Ala.
Scott, Dr. D. W. McDonough, Ga.
Scott, James Armstrong, Cora, Ga.
Tadlock, T. H., Noah, Ind.
Taylor, Mrs. Lillie, Hawesville, Ky.
Thrasher, Alonzo, Covington, Ky.
Thrasher, Mrs. Augustus, Atlanta, Ga.
Thrasher, B. E., Watkinsville, Ga.
Thrasher, Carroll, San Francisco, Cal.
Thrasher, C. B. Dade City, Fla.
Thrasher, Barton, Quitman, Ga.
Thrasher, Mrs. Bettie, Jacksonville, Fla.
Thrasher, Charles, Wheeling, W. Va.
Thrasher, Charles, Indianapolis, Ind.
Thrasher, Mrs. David, Lake City, Fla.
Thrasher, David, Milldale, Ky.
Thrasher, David, Atlanta, Ga.
Thrasher, D. W. Covington, Ky.
Thrasher, D. B., Jacksonville, Fla.
Thrasher, Mrs. David Hughey, Hernando, Fla.
Thrasher, Judge D. O., Dade City, Fla.
Thrasher, Eli, Lewiston, Mo.
Thrasher, Eli T., Lewisport, Ky.
Thrasher, Edmond, Watkinsville, Ga.
Thrasher, Elias, Florence, Ala.
Thrasher, Rev. G. B., Beattyville, Ky.
Thrasher, F. G., Parisburg, Va.
Thrasher, Dr. G. W., Hillsboro, Ala.
Thrasher, Grafton, Covington, Ky.
Thrasher, J. Q. A., Springwood, Va.
Thrasher, J. H., Demossville, Ky.
Thrasher, I. C., Watkinsville, Ga.
Thrasher, F. A., Iola, Kas.
Thrasher, James M., Winigan, Mo.
Thrasher, James Cloud, Jacksonville, Fla.
Thrasher, Jesse S., Chattanooga, Tenn.
Thrasher, Joel F., Hannibal, Mo.
Thrasher, Josiah.
Thrasher, John, Shelbyville, Ind.
Thrasher, John.

Thrasher, John, Petri, Ky.
Thrasher, Jno. B.
Thrasher, John, Groves, Ind.
Thrasher, John.
Thrasher, Dr. J. D., Forest Hill, W. Va.
Thrasher, John F., Browage, Mo.
Thrasher, John F., Lewisport, Ky.
Thrasher, John J., (Cousin John) Dade City, Fla.
Thrasher, John P., Groves P. O. Ind.
Thrasher, John R., Brashear, Mo.
Thrasher, John S.
Thrasher, John W., Quitman, Ga.
Thrasher, Dr. Marion, San Francisco, Cal.
Thrasher, Matilda, Shelbyville, Ind.
Thrasher, Mason, Sherman, Texas.
Thrasher, Melvin, Shelbyville, Ind.
Thrasher, Milton B., Shelbyville, Ind.
Thrasher, Nelson, Demossville, Ky.
Thrasher, Reuben, Collay, Pa.
Thrasher, R. E., Savanna, W. Va.
Thrasher, Sarah Murray, San Francisco, Cal.
Thrasher, Samuel, Lewisport, Ky.
Thrasher, Stephen, Lewisport, Ky.
Thrasher, Hon. Stephen, Oak Lawn, Miss.
Thrasher, Mrs. S. F., Lewisport, Ky.
Thrasher, Stephen.
Thrasher, Thomas, Lewisport, Ky.
Thrasher, Thomas.
Thrasher, Dr. T. H., Watkinsville, Ga.
Thrasher, Thomas T., Conyers, Ga.
Thrasher, William Franklin, Lewisport, Ky.
Thrasher, William L., Greentown, Ind.
Thrasher, Dr. W. R., Burkesville, Ky.
Thrasher, William W., Noah, Ind.
Thrasher, William, Burlington, Ia.
Thrasher, William, Indianapolis, Ind.
Thrasher, Mrs. Wilson, Montgomery, Ala.
Thrasher, W. E., Dade City, Ala.
Thrasher, Thomas, Dayton, Ohio.
Thrasher, Woodson Walker.
Thrasher, Professor William M., Irvington, Ind.
Thrasher, Dr. Wade, Indianapolis, Ind.
Thrasher, William, Montgomery, Ala.
Turner, Oscar, Eu Clair, Wis.
Vandegriff, James, Cora, Ga.
Vandegriff, Joseph, Cora, Ga.
Vandegriff, John, Cora, Ga.
Vandegriff, W. C., Lithonia, Ga.
Vandeman, Sarah Thrasher, Denver, Col.
Vineyard, Dock, Forest Hill, W. Va.
Weir, Alice Thrasher, Acton, Ind.
Williams, Maggie, Shelbyville, Ind.

www.ingramcontent.com/pod-product-compliance
Lightning Source LLC
Chambersburg PA
CBHW021946160426
43195CB00011B/1237